FRENCH FOOD
AT HOME

FRENCH FOOD
AT HOME

Laura Calder

WM

WILLIAM MORROW

An Imprint of HarperCollinsPublishers

HarperCollins books may be purchased for educational, business, or sales promotional use. For information please write: Special Markets Department, HarperCollins Publishers Inc., 10 East 53rd Street, New York, NY 10022.

First William Morrow Cookbooks paperback edition published 2005

Designed by Leah Carlson-Stanisic

The Library of Congress has catalogued the hardcover edition as follows:

Calder, Laura.
French food at home / Laura Calder.
p.   cm.
Includes index.
ISBN 0-06-008771-4 (hc.)
1. Cookery, French.   I. Title.

TX719.C22   2003
641.5944—dc21   2002067782

ISBN 0-06-008772-2 (pbk.)

05 06 07 08 09 ❖/QW 10 9 8 7 6 5 4 3 2 1

In memory of my great-aunt Helen Patterson Regan
and for one of the great heroes of my life,
Virginia Tufts Pickett

CONTENTS

ACKNOWLEDGMENTS

*M*any people in France were generous in sharing recipes and good kitchen advice. I am especially indebted to Léon Bernard and Gigi Burland, Chef Pascal Barbot, Chef Marie-Sophie Picard, Chef Randall Price, Marc Benoît, and Ivan Simmonds. With recipe testing, my friends Bridget Oland, Ivan Simmonds, Cathy Grant, and Irene Miller were especially helpful. The taste testers deserve recognition too (it wasn't always a desirable job); I thank all my feasting friends in Paris, especially Christian Bourbonnais Hyde, Philippe Fontes, and Natasha Boswell, who among them were force-fed just about everything.

On the writing and production side, I thank my agent Doe Coover, and everyone at the Doe Coover Agency, for helping me get my idea straight in my own head and helping me to express it the best way possible. I also thank Doe for pairing me with my editor, Harriet Bell at HarperCollins, who always made time for my questions and whose clear vision and sensitivity made this book what it was meant to be. Thank you.

Before a book is started, before the idea even enters your head, there is often someone behind you saying, "You can do this. Go. Go. Go!" For me, that person was Antonia Allegra; I am grateful to her for so much. I also give special thanks to Randall Price and Philippe Fontes for their steadfast friendship and to Christian Bourbonnais Hyde for his support. Finally, I thank my family, including my grandparents who are no longer alive to see this book; it is they who gave me my love of food and my love of language, and they who cheered me on the longest.

INTRODUCTION

French food is, above all, a state of mind: caring about the quality and freshness of ingredients, delighting in the kitchen rather than dreading it, and indulging in the social and sensual life of the table. It isn't just about starred restaurants, professional culinary textbooks, and peasant traditions. My experience of French cooking has been largely in home kitchens, including my own. I have gained skills and a useful repertoire, but more than that, France has taught me to slow down, to cook and eat as though it mattered, to make it matter. And that attitude is the most important thing to take away with you. You have your own ingredients to be proud of wherever you live. French cooking can suggest ways to bring out the best in them. French eating can show you a lifestyle for savoring them more fully. That is what *French Food at Home* is all about.

I also wanted to show you how liberating French cuisine can be for the home cook, how there is room for personal expression, how it is accessible, and how it has evolved to suit modern tastes. My way of doing that is by giving you a picture of life in my own kitchen in France (minus the flops) through a collection of recipes that I have learned to make here. They range from easy to less so, from fast to slow, from traditional to contemporary, and they are set in the context of dinner by courses, so that you can plan a meal as basic or elaborate as you like.

APÉRITIFS

The French approach the apéritif hour with an ease and simplicity well worth adopting: all the effort it has to take is opening a packet of nuts and popping a cork. I'm all for this because, as the cook, it means I get to stop working and join the party, rather than transform myself into a cocktail waitress.

The drinks are simple. Usually, a bottle is opened to share: chilled rosé, white, or sparkling wine. A bottle of cassis may be on offer too, in case someone wants a kir. And if there is a specialty of the region, such as pastis or Suze, that may be served as well. I'm not saying there aren't people out there who reach for whiskey or port (yes, port before dinner), not to mention their collection of shady, untouched bottles brought back from travels. But in the general run of things, variety is not a requirement; not, in fact, necessarily even desirable.

The same goes for the food accompanying those drinks. A bowl of pistachios or potato chips is usually it. Or there might be a dish of olives or radishes, maybe a plate of thinly sliced artisanal sausage. Those are my staples. If I'm in the mood, I might make Mayonnaise and Crudités or Gougères. And, on special occasions, I can be inspired to go a bit further and present, perhaps, gratinéed Hot Mussels or Herb Beignets.

But involved hors d'oeuvre are the exception for me, not the rule. And I don't bring out tray upon tray either; I choose one thing and try to do it nicely. The point of the apéritif is to take a breath and make the transition between the business of life and the relaxed enjoyment of the meal to come. You want to excite the appetite too, not extinguish it. I figure, all guests really want is a salty nibble so their heads don't spin from drinking on an empty stomach. And all the cook wants (and deserves) is a chance to sit down.

SPICED ALMONDS

[Makes 1 cup/150 g]

Whatever amount of spiced nuts you make you're going to eat, so if I look cheap with my quantities, consider it an act of benevolence, not parsimony. Feel free to vary the spices depending on what you have around, and be sure to judge amounts according to your own taste, because spices vary in strength depending on their quality. As for the nuts, hazelnuts or pecans are nice alternatives. I wouldn't go mixing them, though; somehow it reminds me of those tacky mail-order bridge mixes from the 1970s.

1 cup/150 g whole almonds, with their skins on
2 teaspoons peanut or vegetable oil
1 to 2 teaspoons paprika
1 to 2 teaspoons cumin
A good pinch of chili powder
Salt and pepper

Toast the nuts in a dry frying pan over medium heat, stirring more or less constantly and keeping a hawk's eye on them, because they can burn easily. These will take about 20 minutes to darken like aged oak and emit a nutty, roasted perfume.

When the almonds are quite dry, add the oil and toss the pan. Now add the spices and seasonings, tossing again to coat. Slide the almonds onto a plate, spreading them out to dry for about 5 minutes. Taste them. Adjust the seasoning. Pour into a bowl and serve, or keep in an airtight container for a few hours.

SEASONED OLIVES

[*Makes 1 cup/160 g*]

*I*t may be only a small gesture but at some level this recipe is about control. Yes, you can buy olives already seasoned. You can buy a lot of things ready-made and you know what most of them are like. I'd rather decide for myself on the quality of oil, on the mix of herbs, on the balance of seasonings. And I want the freedom to flavor my olives this way one week—slick, herb-flecked, lemony, and salty—and the next week with a scattering of chile peppers, or with a few feathers of fennel or dill. Maybe I want green olives this time and black the next. Besides, I like looking at what's on the table and being able to say, "I did that."

1 cup/160 g olives
¼ cup/60 ml high-quality olive oil
4 garlic cloves, crushed
1 tablespoon lemon juice, or to taste
Grated zest of 1 lemon
2 teaspoons chopped thyme leaves
1 bay leaf
Freshly cracked black pepper

Mix all the ingredients in a bowl so that the olives are well coated, slick, and glistening with marinade. Taste and adjust the seasonings. Spill the olives into a jar and screw on the cap. Refrigerate 3 to 5 days.

Serve. And when all the olives are eaten, marinate a piece of meat in the remaining oil, or use it in salad dressing; whatever you do, don't throw it out.

THYME LICKS

*T*hese are for sucking, not eating, which might strike some as odd. The recipe comes from the owners of a shop in my neighborhood called Alicante, which specializes in oils from all over the world, in particular, very fine olive oils. You just pick up a tiny branch, suck off the herb-perfumed oil, and then discard the twig like a pit. Maybe give a demo so that nobody starts choking them down whole.

1 bunch thyme
Very good olive oil
Fleur de sel

Snip the thyme into small, lollipop-sized brooms. Dip them in the olive oil, lay them on a plate, and refrigerate. The oil will set on the branches. Pull from the fridge just before serving and sprinkle with salt.

WAYS WITH TAPENADE

[*Makes about 1¼ cups/375 ml*]

Fresh tapenade can knock you backward. But wait a day and the flavors mellow to make a still perky, but no longer puckering, shimmering onyx spread. The simplest thing is to toast slices of French bread, pile on tapenade, and serve. A snazzier approach is to roll a sheet of puff pastry into a rectangle less than ¼ inch/½ cm thick, then spread on tapenade and roll it up into a log as you would pinwheel cookies. Put the log in the freezer to stiffen a bit, then slice off thin, even spirals and lay them on an oiled baking sheet. Bake in a 450°F/230°C oven until golden, about 10 minutes. Finally, another tapenade trick comes from La Madeleine, a Michelin-starred restaurant in Burgundy. Chef Patrick Gaultier bakes tapenade crisps, which hold together magnificently and can be cut into a variety of shapes for serving with drinks, or with soup or salad. For those, heat the oven to 375°F/190°C. Beat together 1 cup/200 g smooth tapenade with ¾ cup/90 g flour and 2 teaspoons lightly beaten egg white until completely smooth. Spread on a nonstick baking sheet about ⅛ inch/3 mm thick. Grate Parmigiano-Reggiano over and bake 10 to 12 minutes. Then slide off onto a board for cutting.

Of course tapenade is by no means limited to the apéritif hour. Pack it onto fish or chicken and bake, toss it with pasta, stir it into vinaigrette or mayonnaise, or mash it with the yolks of hard-boiled eggs and stuff them back into the whites. The next idea is yours.

3 cups/500 g black or green olives, pitted and chopped
6 to 8 tablespoons capers, rinsed and drained
8 to 12 anchovy fillets, drained
4 to 6 garlic cloves, crushed
½ cup/125 ml olive oil
1 lemon, halved
Pepper

Pound the olives together with the capers, anchovies, and garlic. I like the romantic toil of a mortar and pestle myself, but you can just whiz everything in a food processor if you'd rather. Blend in the olive oil, adding it in a thin drizzle. Squeeze in lemon juice to taste. I always grind in some black pepper too. No salt, obviously.

EGGPLANT TARTINES

[Makes about 1½ cups/375 ml]

To call squished-up eggplants "caviar," as people often do, is a little exaggerated, but I do understand the impulse to raise the dish above a name like "mush." This thick, smooth purée of oven-roasted eggplant kicking with garlic and lemon is too good for that. And I don't just mean cold and smeared on French bread toasts, but also warm as an accompaniment for, say, lamb. Now, a word about the garlic. I use raw here because I like its sharp freshness. A friend of mine, however, thinks I should be telling you "roasted," which is more on the mellow side and which she prefers. Try my way one time and hers the next and see who you side with. My method is below. For her way, add a head of separated and unpeeled garlic cloves to the pan to roast along with the eggplant. Then carry on with the recipe, adding the soft, squeezed-out pulp instead of the raw.

1 large eggplant (about 1 pound/500 g)
1 to 2 tablespoons olive oil, plus more for brushing
2 garlic cloves, chopped fine or crushed
Lemon juice to taste
Salt and pepper
1 tablespoon chopped fresh parsley

Preheat the oven to 400°F/200°C. Halve the eggplant lengthwise. Score the flesh in crisscrosses without piercing through to the skin. Set flesh side up in a baking dish and brush lightly with olive oil. Bake until soft, 45 minutes to 1 hour.

Scoop out the pulp and purée with the garlic, using an immersion blender. Whisk in the oil. Season with lemon juice, salt, and pepper. Stir in the parsley and refrigerate until serving. Serve on toasted slices of French bread.

CELERY RADISH BUTTER SALT

[*Serves 4*]

*T*he title sums it up. But you'll have to prepare a plate to prove to yourself that with really good ingredients, something this simple is beautiful, and it's enough. The point of the butter is to soften the taste of sharp radishes, but it's not needed if you can find a small, young mild variety. Also, *fleur de sel*, a special French sea salt, is a treat here, worth keeping an eye out for.

1 bunch radishes
2 bunches celery
Coarse sea salt, preferably *fleur de sel*
Unsalted butter

Trim the tops from the radishes, leaving on a bit of green for a colorful handle. Trim the celery, removing the outer ribs for another use. Separate the pale, tender inner stalks and leave them in their elegantly long state.

Arrange the vegetables on a serving platter. Put the salt in one small dish and the butter in another, with a knife for spreading. Serve all together.

MAYONNAISE AND CRUDITÉS

[*Makes about 1 cup/250 ml*]

The crudités are for the mayonnaise, really, not the other way around. You can't fathom how good the homemade stuff is until you taste it. And, frankly, peeling carrots and breaking up cauliflower for dipping is a more challenging task. Here we have plain mayonnaise. If you plan to flavor it, do so before adding the oil. Add a spot of curry powder, a kerplop of Dijon mustard, a squirt of tomato paste heightened with a pinch of cayenne, or a smear of crushed garlic. Another time, try adding a finely chopped herb: tarragon, parsley, basil, whatever suits your state of mind. A favorite of mine is mayonnaise made with walnut oil. I realize that the world is olive oil mad at the moment, but I find its flavor violent in mayonnaise. If you insist on it, use maybe only one part olive oil to two parts grapeseed or another plain oil.

Various raw vegetables, such as carrots, cherry tomatoes, green beans, button
   mushrooms, red pepper, cauliflower, and cucumber
2 egg yolks, at room temperature
Salt and pepper
2 teaspoons white wine or tarragon vinegar
1 cup/250 ml grapeseed or peanut oil
Lemon juice to taste

Wash and cut a colorful heap of assorted raw vegetables. Arrange on a platter. Whisk the yolks in a bowl together with the salt, pepper, and vinegar. Add the oil in a slow, thin stream, whisking constantly until thick. Season with lemon juice, and add more salt and pepper if needed. Serve with the crudités.

CHAMPAGNE HERB BEIGNETS

[*Makes 30 to 50 beignets*]

*D*on't let the word "Champagne" scare you off, because Perrier, beer, hard cider, soda water, anything that bubbles, really, works just fine in place of sparkling wine. In other words, use anything you've got just for a chance to make these deep-fried leaves, because they are so beautiful you won't believe it. And, while you're frying the beignets, also show yourself the exquisiteness of a plain deep-fried leaf. Without dipping it in batter, plunge a basil leaf into the hot oil for just a few seconds until it crisps to tissue-paper delicacy and turns translucent, electric green. A few fried herbs scattered over the beignets for garnish is stunning. And, by the way, when you're done frying, don't throw out the oil. Let it cool, strain it to get the bits out, funnel it back into the bottle, and label "for frying." You can use it a few more times.

¾ cup/100 g all-purpose flour
⅔ cup/85 g cornstarch
½ teaspoon salt
¾ cup/175 ml Champagne, cider, beer, or sparkling water
4 cups/1 l peanut oil
30 to 50 sage, mint, or basil leaves

Put the dry ingredients in a bowl. Whisk in the sparkling wine and let the batter sit for 30 minutes.

Heat the peanut oil in a deep-fryer or high-sided saucepan until spitting hot, about 375°F/190°C, or until a little rip of bread sizzles on contact and soon turns color. Dip the leaves in batter, one by one, and drop them carefully into the oil. They shouldn't sink (if they do, the oil isn't hot enough, so wait); you want them to sizzle and start puffing up immediately. Turn a few times with tongs so they color evenly. When they're golden, remove to paper towels to drain, and immediately sprinkle with salt. Serve in a generous, rustic pile on a plate, garnished with a few plain fried leaves if you like.

FLOWER PRESS POTATO CHIPS

[*Serves 4 to 6*]

I'm not above a bag-o'-chips, mind you. These are simply a reminder of the true and inherent elegance of potato chips, which is easy to forget if all we ever eat are the bought kind, devoured by the fistful from crinkly bags. By parsley leaf, I also mean chives, thyme, basil, cilantro especially, whatever herb you have around and want to taste in your chip.

4 to 6 starchy potatoes
A handful of flat-leaf parsley leaves
4 cups/1 l peanut oil
Coarse salt, preferably *fleur de sel*

Cut the potatoes into paper-thin slices, preferably with a mandoline. Do not rinse them: they're naturally full of starch and water, which act as edible glue. Stick the slices together in twos with a parsley leaf between, so that the leaf looks like a pressed flower behind waxed paper.

Heat the oil in a fryer (which can be as basic a contraption as a high-sided saucepan). You want the oil at 375°F/190°C, or hot enough to make a chip sizzle on contact and start coloring. If the chip doesn't make noise or if it sinks, the oil isn't hot enough, so give it another minute.

Fry the chips in batches until crisp, 2 to 3 minutes. Don't overcrowd them in the oil, or they won't crisp properly. Remove the chips to paper towels to drain and sprinkle immediately with salt. Serve straight away.

FRENCHIFIED POPCORN

[Makes 1 big bowl]

$\mathcal{I}$f you ever saw the movie *The Gods Must Be Crazy*, then you remember what strange things can happen when something from one culture suddenly falls from the sky into another. Popped corn, to us, is the snack of American movie theaters. But give a bag of kernels to a Frenchman . . .

½ cup/125 g unsalted butter, more if you like
About 3 garlic cloves, crushed
3 tablespoons grapeseed oil
1 cup/200 g popcorn kernels
2 tablespoons *herbes de Provence*
Celery salt to taste
Salt

Melt the butter with the crushed garlic, ever so gently, in a small saucepan. Remove from the heat and set aside to infuse. Heat the oil in a large pot. Add the popcorn, tossing to coat. Cover, and shake the pan over high heat until all the corn has popped. Remove from the heat. Pluck the garlic cloves from the butter and pour over the popcorn. Toss. Add the *herbes de Provence* and plenty of celery salt. Toss again. Season with regular salt to taste, and serve.

GOUGÈRES

[Makes 40 to 50 gougères]

*I*f you're new to choux pastry, as I was before I came to France, then read-ing the method you'll never believe it can work. But it does. Things may get a bit splattery the first time, but there can be great joy in mess making. Besides, all else ceases to matter when you peek into the oven at your wee blobs of paste and see them puffing into perfect, airy, golden balls. The traditional cheese for gougères is Gruyère, but I don't see why you couldn't use cheddar, or blue cheese, or Parmigiano-Reggiano, or whatever else. Also, paprika and celery salt are wor-thy additions.

⅓ cup plus 1 tablespoon/100 g unsalted butter
½ teaspoon salt and pepper
1 cup/125 g all-purpose flour
3 eggs
4 ounces/100 g Gruyère cheese, coarsely grated or very finely diced
Milk for brushing

Preheat the oven to 375°F/190°C. Put the butter in a heavy saucepan with 1 cup/ 250 ml water and salt and pepper. Bring to a boil and pull from the heat. Add the flour all at once, and beat until smooth with a wooden spoon. The mixture will pull away from the sides of the pan and form a ball. Put the pan back on low heat and beat for a minute or so to dry the paste somewhat. Remove from the heat and let cool about 3 minutes.

Add the eggs one at a time, beating vigorously with a wooden spoon after each addition. What you want is a smooth, soft, glossy paste that falls easily from the spoon. Stir in the cheese. Using a pastry bag, pipe 1-inch/2.5-cm rounds onto a buttered baking sheet, or simply drop the mixture by spoonfuls. Brush with milk, so they will emerge golden. Bake until puffed up and nicely browned, about 25 minutes.

PARMESAN TUILES

[*Makes 12 to 15 tuiles*]

hese tuiles are quite rich, so two per person is not a miserly serving. You don't have to serve them as an appetizer either. Bent into a rounded tuile ("tile") shape, which is to say slapped onto a rolling pin the instant you can move them so that they cool into a curve, you can serve a scoop of savory sorbet in them or a tiny salad, or perch them on a mound of Spring Ragout (page 171). For drinks, just arrange some on a plate and pass them around. And, incidentally, you must, if you value your sanity, use a nonstick baking sheet so these slip off easily. Another option, especially if you're only making a few, is to do them on top of the stove in a nonstick frying pan.

2 cups/200 g freshly grated Parmigiano-Reggiano

Preheat the oven to 400°F/200°C. On a nonstick baking sheet, make mounds of the grated cheese, about 2 tablespoons each. Flatten them into cookie-shaped rounds. Bake until the cheese is melted and bubbling, 3 to 5 minutes. Remove from the oven and let cool for a minute before slipping off the sheet with a spatula; otherwise, they won't hold together. Don't let them harden too much if you plan to shape them. If you make these early in the day, store in an airtight container until serving so they won't go soggy.

SALT AND PEPPER SHRIMP

[*Serves 4 to 6*]

*H*ere is proof that the only seasonings you ever really need are genuinely good coarse salt and top-notch pepper. People go crazy for shrimp like this. And even though you've tossed them together in seconds right under their noses, they still ogle you in awe and ask you how you made them. I'd lie if I were you.

2 tablespoons olive oil

24 medium shrimp (thawed are fine), peeled

1 teaspoon coarse sea salt or *fleur de sel*

1 tablespoon mixed peppercorns (especially pink and black), cracked

Heat the oil in a nonstick frying pan until spitting hot. Add the shrimp, tossing the pan to coat, then immediately add the salt and pepper. Keep tossing until the shrimp turn pink and curl, 2 to 3 minutes. Slide the pepper-speckled shrimp onto a plate, pierce with toothpicks, and serve straight away.

HOT MUSSELS

[*Serves 4 to 6*]

*T*he advantage of these is that you can assemble the mussels in advance and simply flash them under the broiler at the last minute, either to serve with drinks or as a starter. You may recognize the first part of the recipe as good old *moules marinière,* so obviously if you want to stop the process right there, go ahead. Alternatively, if, the day of making, it's hotter out than you'd expected, maybe instead of grilling you'd rather swap the butter for olive oil, add a nip of vinegar, and turn this into a salad. Say you actually start out with the intention to follow the recipe below, there are still more options. You could use chervil, for example, instead of parsley, and maybe sprinkle over a little anise-flavored liqueur. You could replace half the bread crumbs with ground almonds. Either way, you might like a bit of Parmigiano-Reggiano finely grated over the mussels before broiling. Lime instead of lemon . . . And then, what would happen if a thin slice of chorizo sausage got slipped on top of each mussel, then blasted under the broiler?

½ cup/125 ml white wine
3 shallots, finely chopped
1 bouquet garni (1 bay leaf, 1 thyme sprig, 1 parsley sprig, and 4 peppercorns, tied with string
40 to 50 (1 pound/500 g) large mussels, scrubbed
¼ cup/60 g unsalted butter
2 garlic cloves, peeled
A handful of chopped fresh parsley
1 to 2 tablespoons bread crumbs
Salt and pepper
1 lemon, cut into wedges

Put the wine, shallots, and bouquet garni in a large pot and bring to a boil. Having discarded any open mussels, add the remainder to the pot, cover, and cook until they open, 3 to 4 minutes. With a slotted spoon, remove the mussels to a bowl to cool, discarding any that didn't open. (Strain the liquid and freeze for future fish stock.) Now, pull apart the shells, discarding the tops and keeping the bottoms with the mussels nested in them. Set on a baking sheet.

Preheat the oven to broil. Mash the butter with the garlic and parsley. Smear a little onto each mussel. Sprinkle each mussel with bread crumbs (and grated Parmigiano-Reggiano, if you like, too). Season with salt and pepper. Broil until golden, about 3 minutes. Remove to a platter and serve immediately with the lemon wedges.

DUCK ON A STRING

[*Makes 1 breast*]

*T*his is more than an appetizer, it's a conversation piece. I know a lady who has one of these duck deals perpetually bobbing on her clothesline, and a couple that dangles theirs under an awning by the woodpile. It sounds a bit archaic, maybe, but cured duck is a delicacy. And I think it never hurts to be reminded that patience and fresh air can be cooking methods in their own right. Duck on a String is served in very thin slices, shaved off with your sharpest knife. Serve them on their own, or wrapped around a prune and poked with a toothpick. Or, here's another idea from my ingenious cooking buddy, Ivan: once when he came for dinner (Duck on a String dangling from a finger), he grabbed a pear from the fruit bowl, chopped it fine, and tossed it in olive oil, salt, and pepper, then piled it daintily onto thin slices of French bread, and topped them with curls of sliced duck. What a perfect combination that was. I've since repeated it, tossing the dressed pear slices and duck into salad for a starter, rather than having them on bread.

1 duck breast
Coarse sea or kosher salt
Freshly cracked black pepper

Surround the raw breast entirely with coarse sea salt and leave to sit at cool room temperature overnight.

Remove the duck from the salt and give it a good shake to get most of the grains off. Now, pack on the pepper, pressing it to stick, so that the breast is completely covered. Refrigerate overnight.

Lift the breast from the pepper, letting what clings to it stay clinging. Pierce a small hole at one end to get a string through. Then hang the duck outside in a place with a good current of air but out of the way of rain. Leave it until quite dry, about 7 days. Don't be alarmed by the hard outer skin; the inside will be perfectly tender. Serve in the thinnest possible slices.

French Food at Home

CLEAR TOMATO COCKTAIL

[*Makes 4 cups/1 liter/serves 6 to 8*]

Usually this is served as a sort of chilled consommé, but it holds up better as an alcohol-free apéritif, or even as a palate cleanser between courses, if you're into that kind of thing. It's pure and refreshing, with a surprising concentration of tomato flavor, making ½ cup/125 ml per serving about right. For variety, purée a red pepper, a stick of celery, or a cucumber with the tomato so there's a combination of flavors. Chopped fresh basil or mint is a nice touch too. This apéritif looks nice in a martini glass, but any stemmed glass will do.

4½ pounds/2 kg very ripe tomatoes, chopped
Salt and pepper
Pinch of sugar
6 to 8 small cherry tomatoes, preferably with their green tops

Purée the chopped tomatoes in a blender. Add salt, pepper, and sugar to taste. Set a conical sieve lined with cheesecloth over a bowl and pour in the mixture. Fold the edges of the cloth over to cover. Refrigerate the whole thing overnight to drain.

The next day, you'll find a clear liquid in the bowl underneath. Taste and adjust the seasonings. Pour into small clear glasses, plunk a cherry tomato into each, and serve.

RHUBARB WATER

*H*ere's an elegant and enlivening pale pink drink that's nice to pull out in hot weather. I read that it's meant to be used like cassis: a little in a glass topped up with Champagne. But I find the flavor so delicate I prefer to drink it straight myself, ice cold.

2 pounds/1 kg rhubarb, washed and cut into chunks (frozen is okay)
¾ cup/150 g sugar, more if desired
1 lemon, thinly sliced

Put the rhubarb in a bowl, pour over 4 cups/1 liter boiling water, cover, and leave at room temperature. The next day, strain the liquid into a saucepan, discarding the rhubarb, add the sugar and lemon, and bring to a boil. Boil 5 minutes. Cool. Strain into a bottle, and cork. Serve ice cold. Keeps about a week.

ORANGE PEEL WINE

*S*ome people flinch at the thought of altering wine in any way, but this *vin au pelures d'oranges* is worth the sacrifice, if you have to think of it that way. I first had it before dinner at Chef Michel Bras' restaurant in the Aubrac, a region in central France. It turned out to be the prelude to the most memorable meal of my life, one that changed the way I felt about food forever. So I have a strong attachment to this recipe, based on Michel Bras' own. The only trouble is that I don't know what wine he used. I've had good results with Muscadet, but any good dry white will do.

One 750-ml bottle dry white wine
1 medium organic orange
⅓ cup/65 g sugar
8 coriander seeds

Open the wine. Pour out half a cup to enjoy while you carry on with the recipe: a bit has to come out, or the bottle will overflow when you add the other ingredients.

Shave the zest from the orange with a vegetable peeler. Remove every trace of the bitter white pith from the back with a sharp knife. Poke the orange zest into the bottle of wine. Funnel in the sugar. Drop in the coriander seeds. Recork the bottle. Turn it upside down and right side up a few times until the sugar has dissolved. Refrigerate 1 week, giving the wine a shake once a day.

Strain into a carafe and serve well chilled.

WINTER WINE

[*Makes about 3 cups/750-ml (1 bottle)*]

*V*in chaud, or hot wine, is just the sort of thing that plucks at my northern heartstrings and makes me feel homesick for Canadian winters. No, I am not just saying that; I like my annual dose of snow and ice. I especially like it when I'm gazing out at those razor-edged, blasting swirls of whiteness from the snug indoors, and when I have a mug of this mulled wine cupped between my thawing paws.

One 750-ml bottle red wine
¼ cup/50 g sugar
1 cinnamon stick
4 cloves
1 star anise
1 strip orange zest, with any pith removed
Lemon slices for serving

Pour the wine over the sugar in a nonreactive saucepan. Stir to dissolve. Add all the other ingredients apart from the lemon slices and heat the wine gently to the boiling point. Lower the heat, cover, and simmer 5 to 10 minutes. Strain and serve with a lemon slice in each glass.

FIRST COURSES

I like a starter. Even a small fennel salad has the civilizing effect of slowing a meal's pace, so we can ease into dinner, relaxed, rather than shovel our way blindly, frantically through it.

Some worry that adding a first course means there will be too much to eat, but slipping an element out of the main course and serving it beforehand solves the problem. For example, instead of having meat-starch-two-veg for the main part of dinner, serve the meat and vegetables in the main and have pasta to start. Or, take away a vegetable from the main course and offer a stuffed tomato or a fan of asparagus first.

My starters are usually quite small, just enough to sharpen the senses and get everyone impatient for what comes next, like Beet Stacks or Langoustines in Sea Cream. Sometimes, when I want to entertain friends with a long and lingering dinner, I make a series of starters, say three or four, and serve no main course at all. Ghost Soup, Soft Herb Eggs, Smoked Trout Rösti, and green salad would be a nice lineup. This kind of thing takes work; I won't pretend otherwise. But, guests love the tasting menu variety.

Do keep an eye out throughout the book for other recipes that can easily become starters. Savory Carrot Cake, Eggs Slowly Scrambled, and Spring Ragout are a few of my very favorites. Likewise, several recipes in this chapter, such as Apple Rabbit Compote, Blue Cheese Pasta, and Burgundy Eggs, make perfect light lunch and supper dishes.

GOAT'S CHEESE TOMATOES

[*Serves 4*]

*Y*ou can but love the contrasts here: crisp, golden croûtes; hot, slouching tomatoes plumped with herb-flecked cheese; a colorful tangle of cool textured greens shimmering with vinaigrette. Obviously it doesn't need additional garnish, but sometimes when I'm going all out I make a *coulis* by puréeing and straining the insides and leftover bits of tomato. Then, when I serve the salad, I drizzle the pinkish red sauce around the plate and splash on a few yellow drops of olive oil. This is nice too, if you have the patience, with cherry tomatoes; for four people, you need twelve, and you arrange three around each salad.

4 medium tomatoes

Salt and pepper

4 slices French bread

3 tablespoons olive oil, plus more for brushing

1 garlic clove, halved

8 ounces/250 g fresh goat's cheese

A handful of chopped fresh herbs, such as parsley, chervil, thyme, and
  rosemary

4 small handfuls mixed greens (preferably including arugula and frisée)

2 teaspoons balsamic or sherry vinegar

Shave a sliver from the very bottom of each tomato so they'll sit steady and not roll over. Then slice off the tops and carve out the insides with a spoon. Sprinkle the tomatoes inside with salt, and set them upside down on paper towels to drain for about 20 minutes. Pat the inside dry.

Preheat the oven to 450°F/230°C. Brush both sides of the bread with olive oil, rub with the split garlic clove, and place on a baking sheet.

Mash the goat cheese together with the herbs and pepper. Stuff each tomato with the mixture and set one on each piece of bread. Bake until the tomatoes are hot, with slumping shoulders, and the cheese is golden on top, 20 to 25 minutes.

To serve, toss the greens with the oil and vinegar. Season with salt and pepper, and arrange on four plates. Take the tomato croûtes from the oven and nudge one up against each salad.

BACON AND HAZELNUT LEEKS

[*Serves 4*]

*W*arm leeks napped in smoky bacon cream with the crack of nuts in their bite is one of the first things I start craving when I sniff the air, suddenly frost-edged, and know that autumn is striding through, with winter barking at her heels. Now this is one of those recipes that should never be corseted by recipe form, because leeks come in all sizes and this means that you may need more or less bacon, more or fewer nuts, plus or minus a glug or two of cream. So toy with the amounts: they're not absolute. To help with your planning: in the case of baby leeks, estimate two to three per person; with medium narrow leeks, as I indicate below, one per person is fine; and if you should find yourself facing leeks of thug-like thickness, peel off a few outer layers to narrow them down, and then halve lengthwise once cooked, planning one-half per person.

4 medium leeks
4 tablespoons coarsely chopped hazelnuts
4 to 6 strips bacon, cut into pieces
1 tablespoon white wine vinegar
1 cup/250 ml heavy cream
Salt and pepper

Bring a large pot of salted water to a boil. Trim all but an inch of green from the leeks. Wash them thoroughly, tie them in a bunch with string, and plunge them into the boiling water. Cook until tender when pierced with a fork, about 20 minutes. Drain and quickly rinse in cold water to stop the cooking. Drain, remove the string, pat dry, and keep warm.

Meanwhile, toast the hazelnuts in a dry frying pan; set aside. In the same pan, fry the bacon until crisp; set aside. Deglaze the pan with the vinegar, scraping up any good stick-to-the-pan bits. Pour in the cream and boil for a minute or so to reduce to sauce consistency. Season with salt and pepper. Stir in the bacon and nuts.

Place 1 leek on each serving plate, spoon around the sauce, and serve hot.

French Food at Home

ORANGE ASPARAGUS

[Serves 4]

*D*on't hesitate to use this as a side dish; that's where it started. I was picturing it on a buffet table outdoors, somewhere in the neighborhood of a massive ham and an Alsatian Potato Salad (page 154). But then it was so good, fans of spring asparagus with a bright, tangy sauce so delicious I had to fight myself not to drink it, I decided to leave it on its own.

2 pounds/1 kg green or white asparagus
2 juicy oranges
1 heaping tablespoon chopped shallot
2 teaspoons white wine vinegar
1 egg yolk
½ teaspoon Dijon mustard
½ cup/125 ml olive oil
Salt and pepper
Yolks of 3 hard-boiled eggs, crumbled
Parmigiano-Reggiano for shaving

Bring a large pot of salted water to boil. Trim the asparagus and, if it's the thick variety, peel the bottom half of the stalks with a vegetable peeler. Bundle the spears together and tie with string. Cook in the boiling water until tender when pierced with a knife, 8 to 12 minutes, depending on thickness. Drain, rinse the asparagus in ice-cold water to stop the cooking, and remove the string. Wrap in a clean tea towel and set aside.

Remove the zest from 1 orange with a vegetable peeler. With a sharp knife, shave off and discard any bitter white pith on the back. Slice into very fine julienne strips, then dice into fine confetti. Blanch in a saucepan of boiling water for 2 to 3 minutes, then drain.

Combine the shallot and white wine vinegar in a small bowl. Leave to macerate while you squeeze the juice from the oranges. Strain the juice into a saucepan and boil it down to about 3 concentrated tablespoons. Add the juice to the shallot and vinegar, along with the raw yolk, blanched orange zest, and mustard. Whisk to blend. Now whisk in the oil in a thin drizzle. Season with salt and pepper to taste.

Arrange the asparagus on a serving platter. Spoon on a bit of sauce. Scatter over the cooked yolks. Grind on black pepper, then decoratively shave over curls of Parmigiano-Reggiano. Pass around the remaining sauce in a bowl, in case someone wants extra.

BEET STACKS

[*Serves 4*]

*I*f you doubt that beets can pull off elegance, try this: thin ruby disks with a nugget of cheese between, glistening with oil, and necklaced with a dark reduction of vinegar. Below I suggest either fresh goat's cheese and pine nuts, or blue cheese with walnuts, two excellent combinations, and both look stellar with a few strands of arugula or a tangle of frisée tucked alongside. If you're worried about finding a cooked beet, just get a raw one and do it yourself. You simply boil it, unpeeled, for 45 minutes to an hour, until a fork poked in tells you that it's tender.

1 to 2 medium beet(s), cooked
4 ounces/125 g fresh goat's cheese or blue cheese
4 scant tablespoons pine nuts or broken walnuts
⅓ cup/80 ml balsamic vinegar
3 to 4 tablespoons olive oil
Salt and pepper

Peel and thinly slice the beet(s). Choose 8 of the nicest-looking slices, and reserve the remainder for another use. Divide the cheese into 4 pieces, and pinch to soften slightly and shape each into an approximate round. Toast the nuts in a dry frying pan for about 5 minutes, stirring constantly. Boil the vinegar down in a small saucepan by about half, until syrupy.

Place a beet slice in the center of each serving plate. Drizzle on a little olive oil, season with pepper, and top with a nugget of the cheese. Drape a second beet slice over the top, like a floppy sun hat. Scatter a few nuts around. Drizzle with the remaining oil and the reduced vinegar. Season with salt and a grind of pepper. Don't forget the few leaves of arugula or frisée on the side, if you have some, also drizzled with the dressing and seasoned.

ONIONS IN THEIR SKINS

[*Serves 4*]

*H*ere I go pinching another recipe from chef Michel Bras, but the instant I saw these onions I knew I had to make them mine. Bras' recipe specified a type of onion that I couldn't find, so I tried instead with medium-sized red onions; they were fantastic. I also tried plain white, sweet onions, the ones with very thin, papery skins, and they were also good and very pretty. The exact timing depends on the kind of onion you use and how big they are. Be prepared to tack on cooking time accordingly.

4 medium sweet onions
4 handfuls coarse sea or kosher salt
1 teaspoon mustard
1 tablespoon white wine vinegar
1 shallot, finely chopped
1 egg yolk
4 tablespoons walnut oil
Salt and pepper
Coarse sea salt, preferably *fleur de sel*
Freshly cracked black pepper

Preheat the oven to 425°F/220°C. Cut barely a sliver off the bottom of each onion so they'll sit without rolling over, then pierce them in a few places with a sharp knife so they won't burst during cooking. Make four mounds of sea salt in a baking dish and nest an onion in each. Bake 15 minutes. Lower the heat to 325°F/160°C and continue baking for about 1½ hours longer: the precise timing depends on the size of the onions; you want the insides to cook until they're almost applesauce soft.

Meanwhile, make the vinaigrette: Mix together the mustard, vinegar, shallot, and yolk. Whisk in 2 tablespoons water. Add the oil in a thin drizzle, whisking constantly. Season with salt and pepper.

Set the onions on serving plates. Spoon some sauce around each. Garnish with sea salt and freshly cracked pepper. Put the remaining sauce in a bowl and send it around the table so that everyone can slit open their onions and dribble in more.

MUSHROOM TOASTS

[*Serves 4*]

I don't suppose I can use the word "scrumptious" and be taken seriously, but that's what you get when you heap hot, woodsy, meaty mushrooms onto crunchy garlic-rubbed toasts. It's a starter when other people are around, but if I'm alone, I just tilt the whole pan into a high, rubbly heap on my plate, dig in, and call it dinner. Vary the mushroom types, depending on what you can find, and don't worry if all you can get are the button variety. The herb can vary too: tarragon, for example, is good.

1½ pounds/750 g mixed mushrooms, such as button mushrooms, cèpes, and chanterelles
3 tablespoons unsalted butter
12 slices French bread
About 4 tablespoons olive oil
3 to 4 garlic cloves, halved
½ cup/125 ml cream
Salt and pepper
Half a lemon
A handful of chopped fresh parsley

Preheat the oven to broil. Clean, trim, and quarter the mushrooms. Heat 1 tablespoon of the butter in a frying pan until foaming hot. Sauté one-third of the mushrooms until just cooked, 2 to 3 minutes. Remove and set aside. Melt another spoonful of butter and sauté the next third. Finish the remaining mushrooms in the final spoonful of butter. Set the pan aside.

Brush the bread on both sides with olive oil and set on a baking sheet. Toast in the oven for a few minutes, until crisp and golden; turn to toast the other side.

Remove from the oven, and rub the surfaces generously with the garlic. Divide among four plates.

Put all the mushrooms back into the pan and toss to heat through. Stir in the cream and boil for a minute or two, until it has the consistency of a sauce. Season with salt, pepper, and a squeeze of lemon. Remove from the heat and add the parsley. Spoon over the toasts and serve hot.

ARTICHOKES

*I*f you're from the same corner of the continent as I am, then you probably see artichokes as intimidating, reptilian-looking things. But once initiated to what's beneath their carapace and to how easy it is to get at, even we northeastern types start craving them at least once a week, and we crave them with their brims spilling over with thick, lemony hollandaise too. They're best that way: good and messy, pulled apart with the hands, and eaten like a lobster on the *quai*.

2 lemons, halved
4 artichokes
Hollandaise (recipe follows)

Squeeze 1 lemon into a large pot of salted water, throw in the peels, and bring to a boil. Meanwhile, trim the artichokes, rubbing every cut surface with the remaining lemon as you go so they don't turn brown. I recommend a bread knife for cutting artichokes: first cut off the stems and snap off any tough dark green leaves around the base, then slice across the artichokes about one-third of the way down, exposing their inner core.

When the water boils, put in the artichokes, laying a clean tea towel right into the water to cover them and hold them beneath the bubbling surface. Boil until a bottom leaf pulls off easily and the base of the artichokes is tender to a fork, about 40 minutes. Remove and drain.

Pull the inner core from the artichokes and clean out all the hay-like bits, scraping the cavity clean with a spoon. (If they're really hot, rubber gloves can come in handy here.) Set each artichoke on a serving plate and fill with hollandaise. Eat with your fingers, pulling off the leaves and scraping the sauce-dipped ends along your teeth. Then eat the artichoke heart with knife and fork.

HOLLANDAISE

[Makes about 2 cups/500 ml]

This classic sauce is for those artichokes, but as I'm sure you know it's also great on fish, asparagus, poached eggs, and the like. When I made my first hollandaise sauces, I was so afraid of their curdling that I'd always whip them up as thick as mayonnaise, which looked a bit weird, but tasted okay to me. As I grew braver and loosened up, so did the sauce. Now, I make it as it should be: runny-thick, so that it spills off a spoon. Usually I don't start in on it until the artichokes are cooked and drained, but if I'm early, I let the pan of sauce bob around in a larger pan of warm water to wait. It's fine for a while like that, but too long and the sauce will separate, which doesn't look so great. No problem, though, because it's speedily revived by putting a tablespoon of cold water into a clean bowl and whisking into it the supposedly ruined sauce, added in a thin dribble.

1½ cups/375 g unsalted butter
4 egg yolks
Salt and pepper
Half a lemon

Melt the butter slowly in a saucepan. (Some like to leave it on the heat until it turns hazelnut color.) Skim off any foam that rises to the top. Pour off the clear yellow butter into a bowl, leaving behind the remaining milk solids in the bottom. Wash out the saucepan.

Now put the yolks, 4 tablespoons water, and a pinch of salt into the clean pan. Whisk over medium heat until thick enough that the whisk makes ribbons in it, 3 to 5 minutes. If it gets too hot, you'll make scrambled eggs, so lift the saucepan on and off the heat occasionally while whisking to keep the temperature in check. Remove from the heat and slowly drizzle in the clarified butter, whisking all the while until thickened. Season with salt, pepper, and a few squirts of lemon to taste. If the sauce is too thick, whisk in a little water to thin it out. It should pour off a spoon, not be globby like mayonnaise.

ENDIVE SALAD

[*Serves 6*]

*T*his endive salad is like an open jewel box on a plate, and preparation is simply a matter of chopping, crumbling, drizzling, and sprinkling.

4 large endives, quartered and cored
1 medium beet, cooked, peeled, and diced
6 ounces/175 g blue cheese, crumbled
5 ounces/150 g shelled walnuts, broken up a little
½ cup/125 ml walnut oil
2 tablespoons red wine vinegar or lemon juice
Salt and pepper

Separate the endive leaves and arrange in rings on six plates like spokes on a wheel, around and around to use them all up. Scatter over the beet, blue cheese, and walnuts. Whisk together the oil and vinegar and drizzle it over the salads. Sprinkle with salt and grind over good black pepper. Serve.

FENNEL SALAD

[*Serves 2*]

When I come drooping in the door late, this is a favorite that I make for myself. I never measure the ingredients, just slice the fennel and toss in everything else to taste. It always looks fresh: pale white, flecked with yellow and green. And the light crunch of fennel, zing of lemon, and perk of capers together is revivifying no matter how wiped out you are. If you sauté the fennel in olive oil instead of leaving it raw, this becomes a great bed for grilled fish.

1 large fennel bulb, with lots of fern-like green bits on the shoots
2 tablespoons olive oil
Grated zest and juice of ½ lemon
3 tablespoons drained capers
Coarse sea salt, preferably *fleur de sel*
Pepper

Remove the feathery green bits from the fennel and reserve. Cut off the finger-like shoots: if they look good, slice them and add them to the salad; if they look nasty, chuck them out. Peel the bulb with a vegetable peeler, halve, and slice as thin as you can.

Toss the fennel slices in the oil. Add as much of the lemon juice as suits your taste. Mix in the zest and capers. Season with sea salt and pepper. Now put up your feet and eat the salad with a rip of crusty bread while you think about what you want next.

ABOUT GREEN SALAD

*W*hen I crave relief from things cooked, something healthy and light, green salad starts dinner. You can also follow up a main course with this sort of thing, depending on the menu you're serving. I don't have a recipe exactly, but a few reminders are always helpful.

First, buy high-quality green leaves. Nothing inspires like a farmer's market or market stall offering piles of leafy variety: Romaine lettuce, Boston, butterhead, oak leaf, red oak leaf, iceberg, and lamb's lettuce; frisée; chicory; Belgian endive; spinach; sorrel; beet greens; dandelion; radicchio; arugula. Select a few different types for contrast.

At home, pull the leaves from their stalks (if stalks they have) and put them in a sinkful of ice-cold water to soak clean. Lift from the water and drain. If they're really dirty or impressively slug and earwig ridden, give them another round of spa treatment. Spin the water off, wrap them in a towel, and crisp in the fridge until you're ready to put the salad together. Before serving, tear the leaves into pieces (of manageable size for a fork), and put them in a serving bowl.

Adding herbs will enliven the event: basil, chives, cilantro, dill, flat-leaf parsley, mint, marjoram, tarragon, sage, thyme, rosemary, oregano, lemon verbena, and so on. Celery leaves or spring onion tops are good contributions. And, if ever you can find edible flowers too, their colorful blossoms will turn your salad into a celebration: peppery nasturtiums; heady lavender; geranium varieties with perfumes including lemon, mint, peppermint, almond, and rose; petals from marigolds; pillowy pansies; leaves and petals of just-plucked chrysanthemum; blue borage petals; delicate roses, sweet violets, pink clover, and others.

But remember that a green salad is about the greens. This should harness your choice of dressing, which personally I find best when it's nothing but a veil. Good oil (olive, walnut, hazelnut, peanut, almond, grapeseed, and so on) is essential. The vinegar, too, should be as good as you can get, no matter what the flavor: red wine, white wine, Champagne, cider, balsamic, raspberry, walnut, sherry. Sometimes a good squirt of lemon is all the greens need to add an acidic note.

For more subtlety, try sherry, wine, or vermouth instead. Another trick I sometimes like is adding a small amount of good meat stock for richness. A teaspoon of Dijon mustard often goes into my dressing too, for piquancy, as well as a judicious amount of minced shallot or garlic.

Don't underestimate the value of good salt and pepper. For garnish, I buy the French sea salt called *fleur de sel*. Kosher salt is also good, and in America perhaps easier to buy. If you find it too coarse, simply crush it a little with a mortar and pestle. Pepper, like any spice, is best bought from a reliable grocer. Get whole peppercorns, spill them into a pepper grinder, and grind them fresh over the salad just before serving.

APPLE RABBIT COMPOTE

[*Serves 4*]

*T*his exquisite commingling of flavors, packed into pots, makes a hearty, autumn starter served with country bread and perhaps a bit of chutney. It also makes a fine lunch dish, if you'd rather, and maybe you would if only as an excuse to eat more of it. For lunch, a Green Salad (see page 40) or Fennel Salad (page 39) is all you need with it.

1 tablespoon unsalted butter

1 tablespoon olive oil

4 rabbit legs, split between leg and thigh (about 1⅔ pounds/850 g in all)

1 heaping tablespoon honey

1 cup /250 ml cider

1 onion, finely chopped

2 shallots, finely chopped

4 to 5 garlic cloves

½ celery stalk, finely chopped

1 Granny Smith apple, peeled, cored, and grated

1-inch/2.5-cm piece fresh ginger, peeled and finely chopped

1 teaspoon chopped fresh thyme

1 teaspoon chopped fresh tarragon

1 teaspoon chopped fresh rosemary

2 bay leaves

Salt and pepper

Preheat the oven to 300°F/150°C. Heat the butter and oil in a skillet. Brown the rabbit pieces well on both sides, working in batches if necessary, about 15 minutes. Return all the pieces to the pan and drizzle over the honey. Pour over the cider, scraping up the sticky bits in the bottom of the pan. Stir in the onion, shallots, garlic, celery, apple, ginger, thyme, tarragon, rosemary, and bay leaves. Season with salt and pepper.

Transfer the mixture to a baking dish with a tight-fitting lid. Cover and bake until the meat is falling from the bone, 1½ to 2 hours. Remove the meat from the bones (freeze the bones for stock) and shred with two forks, mashing a bit as you go. Strain the cooking liquid into a saucepan and boil down to 1 cup/250 ml, about 10 minutes. Stir in the meat. Taste, and correct the seasonings. Pack the mixture into ramekins, or into one big bowl. Serve with toasted French bread and a bowl of olives.

BURGUNDY EGGS

[*Serves 6*]

*O*h, how I did not want to make these when I first came to France; I thought nothing on earth sounded quite so vile. But eventually I tried *oeufs en meurette*, brave me, and discovered that I adore them. They're a wintertime thing to eat, filling and old-fashioned, with a rich, burgundy-colored sauce speckled with bright orange carrot dice. I just love what they look like; so delightfully unfashionable. And they don't have to be a starter, two eggs per person makes a perfect supper. Have extra bread on the table for mopping up sauce.

¼ pound/125 g bacon, cut into matchsticks
2 tablespoons cold unsalted butter
1 tablespoon vegetable oil
1 onion, chopped
2 carrots, peeled and finely diced
3 garlic cloves, slightly crushed
1 tablespoon all-purpose flour
1 bay leaf
1 bunch parsley, a sprig or two for the sauce, the rest chopped
2 cups/500 ml red wine
2 cups/500 ml chicken stock
Salt and pepper
¼ cup/60 ml white vinegar
6 very fresh eggs
6 slices country bread, toasted or fried in butter

Fry the bacon in a large sauté pan. Remove and set aside. Wipe out any excess fat, then add a tablespoon of the butter and the oil to heat. Sauté the onion until soft, about 10 minutes. Add the carrots and garlic and sauté about 5 minutes. Sprinkle with the flour, stir to blend, and cook 5 minutes more. Return the bacon to the pan, along with the bay leaf and a branch or two of parsley. Pour over the wine and stock. Boil to reduce almost to a sauce consistency, about 20 minutes.

Remove the parsley, bay leaf, and garlic. Season the sauce with salt and pepper, then whisk in the remaining tablespoon of butter to make it nice and glossy.

Meanwhile, bring 4 cups/1 liter water and the vinegar in a deep skillet to a boil. Stir the water to get a whirlpool going and crack the eggs one at a time into the moving water. Poach until set, about 2 to 3 minutes, turning once with a spoon to wrap the whites a bit around the yolks. Remove to drain on paper towels.

To serve, spoon the hot sauce into soup plates. Set a piece of toast in the center of each, and top with a poached egg. Season with salt and pepper, sprinkle with chopped parsley, and serve immediately.

SOFT HERB EGGS

[*Serves 4*]

*S*oft-boiled eggs are mind-bogglingly good, and with a fine, pale pool of herb sauce spooned in, they are delicate. The idea here is that each person be served a soft egg with its top lopped off, a spoonful of sauce tipped in, and a stack of buttered toast fingers alongside for dipping. I like the fingers rustic looking, so I cut them from a nice country loaf, melt some butter in a pan, and fry them until they're golden on all sides. Three fingers per person is about right.

¼ cup/**60 g** unsalted butter
¼ cup/**60 ml** heavy cream
A heaping ⅔ cup/**24.8 g** chopped mixed fresh herbs, such as parsley, chervil, basil, chives, and tarragon
1 tablespoon lemon juice
Salt and pepper
4 very fresh eggs

Make the sauce as early in the day as you like: Heat the butter and cream together in a saucepan until the butter has melted and the mixture is hot. Remove from the heat and add the herbs and lemon juice. Purée with a blender. Strain into a bowl, if you like. Season with salt and pepper and set aside. Rewarm before serving.

Bring 4 cups/1 liter water to a boil in a deep saucepan. When boiling, remove from the heat and carefully lower in the eggs. Cover and return to the heat for 3 minutes. Remove the eggs and rinse under cold water to stop the cooking.

Set the eggs in eggcups and cut off their tops. Scoop out a small amount of white from the top of each egg, then spoon in a pool of herb sauce. Serve immediately, with toast fingers on the side for dipping, and pass any extra sauce around in a small bowl.

PEA GREEN SOUP

[*Serves 6*]

*I*t depends on the variety of pea in the frozen pea bag, I suppose, but the ones I get make a soup that's bright spring green and bursting with fresh pea flavor. This makes quite small first-course servings, but that's how it should be, just enough to have everyone begging for more.

8 cups/2 pounds/1 kg frozen peas
1 cup/250 ml cream
Salt and pepper

Bring 3 cups/750 ml water to a boil in a saucepan with a pinch of salt. Add the peas, bring back to a boil, cover, and cook until soft, about 10 minutes. Without draining, blend to purée (I just stick my immersion blender right into the pot). Strain through a sieve, pressing to get as much purée through as possible. Stir in the cream, reheat, and season. Serve piping hot.

TOAST SOUP

[*Serves 6 to 8*]

This name, for lack of a better one, because the soup is indefinable. The idea belongs to Chef Pascal Barbot of Astrance restaurant in Paris. Mind you, this recipe isn't quite as he does it, but I would not presume . . . I got the gist from him, though, and then played around until I was happy with my home version. Now, don't tell anyone what it is; serve with your lips sealed. They'll say, "I know this. I know I know this." Then they'll beg you to tell them what you've got in there. Nothing like the power of a good secret.

6 slices smoky bacon
4 cups/1 l chicken stock
About 8 cups/250 g cubed French bread (roughly 1 loaf)
2 cups/500 ml milk, more if needed
2 teaspoons sherry or balsamic vinegar
1 teaspoon Dijon mustard
Salt and pepper
2 tablespoons cold unsalted butter

Fry the bacon until cooked but not necessarily crisp. Pour over the stock, bring to a boil, turn off the heat, cover, and let infuse about an hour.

Meanwhile, toast the bread on a baking sheet in the oven until quite dark, but not burnt. Transfer to a large saucepan.

Strain the stock over the toast, reserving the bacon. Add the milk, vinegar, and mustard and purée until very smooth with an immersion blender. Taste before seasoning with salt and pepper.

Cut the bacon into slivers and refry until crispish. Reheat the soup, whisking in the cold butter at the last minute to give it gloss. Serve piping hot with the bacon bits scattered over.

GHOST SOUP

[*Makes about 4 cups/1 liter/ serves 4*]

Where I read it, I don't know, but the image has stuck with me: consommé as the ghost of a chicken. It's a perfect description for this ethereally light, warm, clear, hauntingly fragrant broth. Apt too, because consommé has so long been out of fashion that to be served it now really is like seeing an apparition. But even if it is ancient, I find consommé unsurpassably chic. I serve it simply, with just a couple of minced shallots or fresh herbs added to the hot pot before ladling it into bowls. If you'd rather a beef consommé, use beef stock and substitute ground beef for the diced chicken.

1 lb/500 g skinless, boneless chicken, diced
1 celery stalk, diced
1 carrot, diced
Green of 1 leek, diced and rinsed
2 medium tomatoes, diced
A handful of parsley, leaves chopped
3 egg whites
6 cups/1.5 l fat-free homemade chicken stock
Salt and pepper

Stir together the chicken, celery, carrot, leek, tomatoes, parsley, and egg whites in a large bowl. Pour the chicken stock into a pot, season with salt and pepper, and whisk in the vegetable mixture. Heat, whisking slowly, until frothy, about 10 minutes. As soon as the stock reaches a simmer, stop stirring. In a few minutes, the egg white mixture will have formed a firm, nasty-looking "raft" on the surface. Make a vent in the raft large enough to get a small ladle through, and continue simmering 30 minutes.

Line a strainer with cheesecloth and set over a bowl. Leaving the raft behind, ladle in the clarified consommé through the hole in the raft and let it strain through. Serve piping hot, with or without garnish.

SCALLOPS IN VELVET

[*Serves 4*]

*B*eautiful soup, this is, and made in minutes. The understated contrast in texture between tender scallops and smooth, barely spiced pumpkin is at once homey and elegant. Scallops do cost a lot, I know, but you need only a few. Replace the pumpkin with squash, such as acorn squash or delicata, if you'd rather. And, if you're braver than I am, try coconut milk in place of regular sometime.

2 pounds/1 kg pumpkin, peeled, seeded, and cut into pieces
½ cup/125 ml cream
½ teaspoon curry powder
Salt and pepper
1 to 2 tablespoons unsalted butter
6 sea scallops, sliced into ¼-inch/5-mm disks

Cook the pumpkin in 2 cups/500 ml boiling water until very tender. Drain, reserving about 2 tablespoons of the cooking water.

Purée the pumpkin and reserved water with a blender. Strain into a saucepan. Stir in the cream. Reheat, cooking the mixture down a bit if it's thin. Stir in the curry, and season with salt and pepper. Strain again if you're a maniac like me about the texture.

Heat the butter to frothing in a frying pan over high heat. Sear the scallops, about 30 seconds per side. You want them to have nice color but not be over-cooked. Season with salt and pepper. Ladle the pumpkin into soup plates. Arrange the scallops in overlapping rings on top. Serve hot.

PISTOU ZUCCHINI RIBBONS

[*Serves 4*]

*T*his is zucchini masquerading as pasta and tossed in the elements of *pistou*, or pesto (garlic, basil, pine nuts, olive oil, and Parmigiano-Reggiano). To get the best "pasta" slices, choose skinny, young zucchini with few seeds. For larger zucchini, halve them lengthwise and peel the ribbons down the narrow side.

4 small zucchini
2 to 3 tablespoons olive oil, more if needed
2 garlic cloves, chopped fine
½ cup/80 g pine nuts, toasted
½ cup/60 g freshly grated Parmigiano-Reggiano
1 large bunch basil, stemmed and chopped
Salt and pepper

Bring a pot of salted water to boil. Peel the zucchini into long strips with a vegetable peeler, or use a mandoline. You'll finish with a pile of vegetable "pasta." Cook the zucchini in the boiling water until just al dente, 1 to 2 minutes. Drain and immediately rinse under ice-cold water to stop the cooking and to preserve the bright color.

Heat the oil gently in a large frying pan. Add the garlic and sauté about a minute. Add the zucchini ribbons, with the pine nuts, cheese, and basil, tossing to coat. Season with salt and pepper. Twist a stack of zucchini onto the center of each serving plate. Garnish, if you like, with additional curls of Parmigiano-Reggiano and a few extra basil leaves. Serve immediately.

BLUE CHEESE PASTA

*T*his is deliciously creamy hot pasta and I love its sharp blue bite, especially when I'm served a little frenzy of it before the arrival of a juicy, pink steak. Besides its gustatory merits, making *pâtes au bleu* is so easy it's almost embarrassing. The French insist on *pâtes fraîches* (fresh egg pasta), but dried works too. For the sauce, use any good blue cheese, such as Roquefort, bleu de Causses, or bleu d'Auvergne.

1 pound/500 g fresh egg pasta, such as fetuccine
½ pound/250 g blue cheese
½ cup/125 ml cream, more if needed
Pepper

Bring a large pot of salted water to boil for the pasta. Melt the cheese, broken into pieces, in a frying pan, and whisk in the cream. Add more if necessary, until you have a smooth fluid sauce the consistency of your liking.

Meanwhile, cook the pasta. Drain, then toss in the "blue." Grind on fresh black pepper. Twist into stacks on plates, and serve hot.

LEMON PASTA

[*Serves 4*]

You'll be hard-pressed to find a lemon sauce quicker than this one: by the time the pasta pot has boiled, the sauce is ready. I make it quite lemony, with a good squirt of lemon juice at the end, and sometimes add extras: shredded smoked salmon, poppy seeds, shredded basil leaves, chopped dill, to name a few options. The sauce can also be served warm over fish, chicken, or rabbit: it's rich in that context, but that never stops me.

2 tablespoons unsalted butter
Grated zest of 4 to 5 lemons
1 cup/250 ml heavy cream
1 ounce/30 g Parmigiano-Reggiano, grated
Salt and pepper
Lemon juice to taste
½ pound/250 g fresh egg pasta

Bring a large pot of salted water to boil for the pasta. While you wait, melt the butter in a saucepan. Stir in the lemon zest. Pour over the cream and bring to a boil. Remove from the heat and add the cheese, stirring to melt. Season with salt and pepper. Add lemon juice to taste.

Cook the pasta. Drain, return to the pot, and toss with the sauce. Divide among four serving plates, garnish as you like (see headnote), and serve immediately.

FRIED CHEESE

[*Serves 4*]

When something sounds as delightfully impossible as this, I can't sleep until I make it. Of course, sometimes things sound impossible for good reason, but that's not the case here. Fried cheese works, and I could eat it all day long. The first time I tried it, two friends were over for dinner; one insisted on adding ground nuts to the crumb mixture for more flavor and the other used a liberal hand with my tandoori spice mix (not very French, but so what). I never make it any other way now, because the results were wonderful, meltingly hot cheese slabs, golden and crunchy in their nutty spiced crumbs. We laid them on plates of lamb's lettuce, garnished with hot cherry tomatoes just sizzled in olive oil for a few seconds to make their skins pop. The whole thing took seconds. Feel free to experiment with the spice (or herb) possibilities, and with the type of ground nuts.

2 tablespoons unsalted butter
½ cup/50 g fine bread crumbs
¼ cup/30 g finely ground hazelnuts or almonds
About 2 teaspoons tandoori spice mix (optional)
8 slices firm white cheese, such as Gruyère, Comté, or Emmental, cut ½ inch/
  1 cm thick
2 eggs, lightly beaten

Heat the butter in a large frying pan until foaming. Combine the bread crumbs and powdered nuts, adding the tandoori spice mix if you like. Dip the cheese "steaks" first into the beaten eggs, then into the crumbs to coat well. Fry gently until the crumbs are golden and the cheese beginning to melt, just a few minutes per side, before they melt too much. Serve straight out of the pan, on salad.

TWO FREE-STYLE TARTS

[Both serve 4]

Almost anything spread on pastry and baked will taste good. So give the leftovers in your fridge a good once over before starting in on tarts. I like the mushrooms of Mushroom Toasts (page 34) as a filling. Caramelized fennel with thyme is decadent. Bacon and sautéed leek with some feta crumbled over . . . It's hard to go wrong. Below, I give instructions for the two kinds I make most often: cherry tomato tartlets, because they're smart looking and fast, and caramelized onion tartlets, which blow me away with goodness when all I've got in the house is a sack of onions. For the tomato tarts, you can always add bits of black olive or a strewing of poppy seeds, or consider a smear of tapenade or pesto underneath the tomato halves. For the onion tarts (which I suggest making slightly smaller, because they are rich) you could add a bit of bacon, or stir in an egg, but to tell the truth, I like them plain. Plain seems to be the whole point. Go ahead and dabble, though, because both tarts are meant to be totally liberating. Even the pastry is cut out and done on a baking sheet—no fitting into little molds required.

CHERRY TOMATO TARTS

Plain Pastry (page 57)
Olive oil for brushing
2 handfuls basil leaves, shredded
⅔ lb/500 g cherry tomatoes, halved
Salt and pepper

Preheat the oven to 400°F/200°C. Roll the pastry to about ¼ inch/5 mm thick, and cut out 4 circles, 5 to 6 inches/13 to 15 cm wide. Grease a baking sheet and set the rounds on it. Brush with olive oil.

Leaving a ¾-inch/2-cm margin around each pastry circle, scatter over the basil and arrange the tomato halves, cut side down, on top. Roll the pastry margin in, scalloping it as you go, to make a lip all around. Season the tarts with salt and pepper. Bake until the pastry is crisp and the tomatoes are hot, about 15 minutes. Serve with a small green salad on the side.

CARAMELIZED ONION TARTS

Plain Pastry (page 57)
½ cup/125 g unsalted butter
About 6 medium yellow onions, sliced
½ cup/125 ml heavy cream
2 teaspoons balsamic vinegar
Salt and pepper
A handful of chopped fresh thyme

Preheat the oven to 400°F/200°C. Roll the pastry to about ¼ inch/5 mm thick, and cut out 4 circles, 4 to 5 inches/10 to 13 cm wide. Grease a baking sheet and set the rounds on it.

Melt the butter in a large skillet, add the onions, and cook, stirring occasionally, until very soft and caramelized, about 30 minutes. Stir in the cream and cook for a few minutes, until the mixture is thick. Add the vinegar and season with salt and pepper. Taste and adjust the seasonings. Stir in the thyme.

Leaving a ¾-inch/2-cm margin around each pastry circle, spoon on the onion mixture. Roll the pastry margin in, scalloping it as you go, to make a lip all around. Bake until the pastry is crisp and the onions browned on top, about 15 minutes.

PLAIN PASTRY

[Makes 1 large tart shell]

*I*n France pastry dough is bound with egg yolk more often than not, like the sweetened kind (page 219). My preference, however, is for this more minimalist egg-free alternative. It seems lighter, flakier, and crispier, plus it's quicker, since no resting time is required before baking. For the record, if ever you're filling a prebaked shell with something liquid, brush the shell with lightly beaten egg white as soon as it's out of the oven; this helps prevent the bottom from going soggy.

1½ cups/200 g all-purpose flour
¼ teaspoon salt
7 tablespoons/100 g chilled unsalted butter, cut into pieces
About 4 tablespoons ice-cold water, more if needed

Measure the flour into a bowl and add the salt. Toss in the butter to coat. Then pinch with your fingers to achieve a fine, crumbly mixture. Alternatively, use a pastry blender. Make a well in the center and add the water. Stir with your fingers, very quickly, to combine, adding more cold water if necessary. Form into a ball. It should hold together, and be neither sticky nor dry. Pat into a disk.

Roll out on a lightly floured board, and line a 9- or 10-inch tart pan.

To prebake the tart shell, preheat the oven to 375°F/190°C. Line the pastry with parchment or foil, and fill with dried beans or other suitable weights. Bake until completely cooked, 15 to 20 minutes.

MARINATED TUNA

[*Serves 4*]

*A*fter muddling around, never satisfied, with different takes on tuna tartare, I went to a friend's house for dinner and was served tuna like this, basically naked. I said, "This is it! This is what I've been trying to do. What's in it?" And he said, "Nothing," which is essentially true. So now, instead of making a blasphemous hash of tuna and chopped bits of this and that, I serve the fish this way, with a minimum of flavorings that complement rather than drown out its perfectly pure, clean taste.

¾ pound/375 g sushi-grade tuna, preferably from the tail end
1 shallot, finely chopped
A large handful of chopped fresh chives
¼ cup/60 ml hazelnut or walnut oil
¼ cup/60 ml olive oil
Freshly cracked black pepper
Coarse sea salt, preferably *fleur de sel*
1 lime or lemon, cut into wedges

Slice the tuna about ¼ inch/2.5 mm thick and put it in a bowl with the shallot and chives. Pour over the oils, grind on pepper, cover, and refrigerate several hours, or overnight.

Arrange the tuna on serving plates, sprinkle with salt to taste, and grind over more pepper. Place a lime wedge or two on each plate for squeezing. Serve with lightly toasted thin slices of French bread.

HERRING AND POTATO TERRINE

[*Serves 6*]

Blanc Mange, by Raymond Blanc, a French chef who has made his career in England, is one of the many hardcover cookbooks for which I traded in all my textbooks at the end of university. Ever since, I've been drooling over a picture in it for "Terrine of Sardines and Potatoes," but only recently was I bold enough to make it. Do I ever wish I hadn't been such a wimp and made it sooner, because it is, just as the picture promised, spectacular. I use herring fillets, because I seem to find them more easily, and actually here I like the smoked kind even better. If you want to use sardines, it might be wise to go by weight when buying, because they tend to be smaller than herring. Blanc garnishes his terrine slices with both a quick cream sauce and a caper vinaigrette. The sauce is made from ¼ cup/60 ml sour cream, 2 teaspoons water, a pinch of both white and cayenne pepper, and a squirt of lemon, all whisked up. For the vinaigrette, whisk together 1 chopped shallot, 1 tablespoon white wine vinegar, and salt and pepper. Whisk in about ¼ cup/60 ml peanut oil, or more to taste, then add a good tablespoon of drained capers and another of chopped parsley. Swirls of those sauces around the edge of a slice of terrine make it lively, chic, and original, really an amazing transformation of ingredients that are traditional and so cheap.

3 large waxy potatoes (about 1 pound/500 g) peeled

4 shallots, minced

3 garlic cloves, minced

1 to 2 rounded tablespoons chopped fresh thyme

6 tablespoons olive oil

Salt and pepper

4 to 5 large fresh herring or sardine fillets (about ½ pound/250 g in total), deboned

Preheat the oven to 375°F/190°C. Line a 4-cup/1-liter terrine mold or loaf pan with a piece of parchment paper. Cut the potatoes into ¼-inch-/5-mm-thick slices, then trim into rectangles that will fit in the mold like tiles; set aside. Combine the shallots, garlic, and thyme in a small bowl.

Smear a little oil around the bottom of the mold. Sprinkle in salt and pepper. You're going to make three layers of potato and two of fish, with the aromatic mixture strewn between, so first lay in an even layer of potato slices. Top with one-quarter of the shallot mixture. Drizzle over one-quarter of the oil. Lay in 2 fish fillets, skin side down. Cut pieces from a third fillet if necessary to fill any gaps. Season well and top with another quarter of the shallot mixture. Drizzle over another one-quarter of the oil. Make another potato layer and season. Carry on layering until the ingredients are used up, ending with potato. Season before covering with foil.

Set the terrine in a baking dish. Pour around boiling water to come about halfway up the sides. Bake until a knife slides easily into the center, about 1½ hours. Remove from the water bath, and cool.

Cut a piece of cardboard slightly smaller than the size of the mold and wrap with foil. Fit it to the top of the terrine and cover with heavy weights (a brick, for example, or soup cans), distributed evenly. Refrigerate overnight with the weights on top so that the terrine sets.

Remove the weights and foil. Run a knife around the edge of the terrine and turn it out. Peel off the parchment. Slice evenly and arrange on serving plates. Drizzle around vinaigrette and sauce (see headnote) and serve.

SMOKED TROUT RÖSTI

[*Serves 4*]

*F*ood like this is beautiful, in the natural kind of way I like. Even though the dish is simple, there's quite a lot going on for the pick-it-apart-and-philosophize types: hot versus cold, smoked versus fried, land versus sea. Since I make it so often, lately I've been embellishing a bit. Very minutely diced leek and a bit of olive oil tossed with the trout add interest. The sauce, instead of horseradish, might be caper and lemon. Also, spicing the rösti takes it to a higher realm; I add celery salt and, well, that tandoori spice again actually, but I'm sure that next time something else will go flying into the mix.

3 to 4 medium waxy potatoes, peeled
1 garlic clove, chopped
A handful of parsley leaves, chopped
1 egg, lightly beaten
Salt and pepper
1 tablespoon vegetable oil
2 tablespoons unsalted butter
½ cup/125 ml sour cream
1 tablespoon bottled horseradish, or more to taste
4 slices smoked trout or salmon (about ¼ pound/125 g total)

Grate the potatoes onto a clean tea towel, then squeeze them in the towel to remove as much water as possible. Shake the potatoes into a bowl and mix with the garlic, parsley, and egg. Season with salt and pepper.

Heat the oil and 1 tablespoon of the butter in a large frying pan until foaming hot. Shape the potato mixture into four pancakes in the pan, pressing them down with a spatula, and dot the remaining tablespoon of butter on top. Fry until the undersides are crisp and well browned, about 5 minutes. Flip and fry until cooked through, about 5 minutes more. Meanwhile, stir together the sour cream and horseradish. Season with salt and pepper.

Place the rösti on serving plates. Arrange the smoked fish in a big curl on top of each. Grind on black pepper. Drizzle over some sauce. Garnish, if you like, with a bit of green, such as chives, or even a small plain salad of arugula.

LANGOUSTINES IN SEA CREAM

[*Serves 6*]

*I*t seems criminal to throw away the shells and heads of langoustines, because they hold exceptional flavor. This recipe uses them to great advantage. Jumbo shrimp work in place of langoustines, but I recommend butterflying them before cooking, by slicing them down the back; they seem more tender that way.

18 langoustines or jumbo shrimp
1 tablespoon unsalted butter
2 shallots, finely chopped
2 garlic cloves, finely chopped
1 bay leaf
2 tablespoons tarragon vinegar
1 cup/250 ml white wine
1½ cups/375 ml light cream
2 egg yolks
Grated zest of ½ lemon
Salt and pepper
1 tablespoon safflower or vegetable oil
Lemon juice to taste
A small handful of finely chopped fresh parsley

Peel the langoustines (or shrimp). Heat the butter in a large pot and add the heads, if using langoustines, and shells. Cook until the tips turn bright red, 2 to 3 minutes. Add the shallots, garlic, bay leaf, and vinegar and cook 1 minute. Pour over the wine and boil 15 minutes.

Strain into a saucepan. You should have about ½ cup/125 ml liquid; if you have much more than that, boil it down to the right amount. Whisk in the cream and bring just to a boil. Reduce the heat and whisk in the yolks one at a time, not allowing the mixture to boil. Cook 2 minutes to thicken slightly. Add the lemon zest, and season with salt and pepper.

In a sauté pan, heat the oil until very hot. Cook the langoustines, tossing the pan, for about 30 seconds. Season with salt, pepper, and a squeeze of lemon. Toss in the parsley. Pile 3 langoustines in the center of each of six soup plates. Reheat the sauce, whisking vigorously until it foams slightly (or use a milk frother, an immersion blender). Ladle the foamy sea cream around the langoustines and serve straight away.

DINNER FAIRLY FAST

I say "fairly fast" because this *is* about cooking, not about assembling a sandwich or a salad, which is all we want to do some nights (and fair enough). But not *most* nights. Especially not when in fifteen minutes to an hour you can prepare something simple, but with substance, that's really worth sitting down to eat.

The trick is having staples in the house, and this is where my enthusiasm for French food really brims. French food is largely about contained variety, and that means you can make a world of dishes with just a few accessible ingredients. Stock the basics: onions, potatoes, eggs, olive oil, capers, Dijon mustard, walnuts, Parmigiano-Reggiano, and so on. That way, through the week, you can simply pick up vegetables and some kind of fish or meat on the way home, then peacefully decide what to do with them once you get there. You'll always have enough to make something good. If you don't believe me, look at recipes like Sea-Salt Salmon, A Good Coffee Chop, and Eggs Slowly Scrambled.

My other weeknight trick, if I don't feel like cooking, is to involve other people. We eat better and we cook better when we're not alone. So, hand off the potato peeling to someone else while you fry the onions. I like to think that more than just me in the kitchen constitutes a party, and spontaneous casual entertaining is the most fun of all, so why wait for the weekend? This chapter has plenty of recipes perfect for occasions like that: Soufflé, Carrot Juice Chicken, Beer Bird, and Herb Lamb, to name a few. They're simple and fast, but looking at them, enjoying them, you'd never know.

EGGS SLOWLY SCRAMBLED

[*Serves 1*]

Someone once told me that eggs should be scrambled at least half an hour to be truly good. So far, I can stretch the cooking time to only twenty minutes, but I am aiming for the long haul. It is, I'll tell you, excellent therapy when you need to play a zombie's role, to stir something endlessly while your glazed, bug-eyed gaze follows a spoon around and around in monotonous circles, and your bruised brain gnaws on a greater problem. Even if you don't solve it within the time limit, the soothing result of soft, smooth, dreamily creamy eggs (with a piece of chervil in the middle to make them pretty, and a few triangles of toast, maybe a curl of smoked salmon too, or bouquets of lamb's lettuce) somehow dilutes one's woes. Not that you should wait for a blast of melancholy to make these. I think they're so worthy of attention, in fact, that I'm proud bringing them out as a starter for a special dinner. If you want to do the same, just multiply the quantities below according to the number of servings.

2 of the freshest eggs you can find
Salt and pepper
2 tablespoons cold unsalted butter
1 tablespoon heavy cream

Whisk the eggs together with salt and pepper. Melt half the butter in the top of a double boiler. Pour in the eggs and cook, stirring constantly with a wooden spoon over the lowest-imaginable heat, until they start to stick to the sides of the pan. Add the cream and keep stirring, scraping up what sticks to the sides and the bottom, until the eggs are thick and set but not stiff. Remove from the heat and beat in the remaining tablespoon butter until creamy. Grind over pepper, and eat immediately.

LEEK TART

[*Serves 4 to 6*]

*T*here's no predicting where or when you're going to stumble upon greatness. The best leek tart I ever ate was on a rainy March lunchtime in the smoke-filled Café de la Préfecture in Dijon. It was so good that I wrote about it in my diary: it had a lot, a lot of leeks in it, cream, and cheese. No wine. No bacon. It was the plainest tart possible, but perfectly delicious. It's worth knowing that the basic formula for any tart is 3 eggs to 1 cup/250 ml milk or cream, and a good handful of cheese. After that anything (or nothing) can go in: sautéed fennel or onions, sliced tomatoes, mushrooms, zucchini, more cheese, diced ham . . .

4 large leeks
1 tablespoon unsalted butter
2 large onions, chopped
1 Plain Pastry shell (page 57), unbaked
1½ cups/150 g grated Gruyère cheese
3 eggs
1 cup/250 ml heavy cream
Salt and pepper
Pinch of nutmeg

Preheat the oven to 425°F/220°C. Trim and discard all but about an inch of green from the leeks. Slice, wash, and drain the rest. Melt the butter in a large saucepan over medium heat and cook the leeks with the onions, stirring occasionally, about 10 minutes. Cover the pan and continue cooking until soft, 10 to 15 more minutes.

Spread the leeks in the tart shell. Top with the cheese. Beat the eggs in a bowl and whisk in the cream. Season with salt, pepper, and the nutmeg. Pour over the leeks and cheese. Bake until the tart has set and is golden on top, about 30 minutes.

POTATO OMELET

[*Serves 2 generously*]

This is the sort of food you can eat three times a week and never tire of. It's rustic, flavorful, and a comfort to cook, with its embracing aromas rising from the pan in a soothing waft: first bacon sizzling, then onion and garlic softening together in butter (or, even better, in duck fat, if you have some of that), then the whole shebang held together by just-stirred fresh eggs. My friend Philippe, master of the potato omelet, also makes another dish along these lines that you'll want to know about. He fries the onion and garlic, then sets those aside while he fries the potatoes crisp and brown. Then the onions and garlic go back into the pan with the potatoes, and he grates cheese (such as Comté, Gruyère, or white cheddar) over the top. He leaves the pan on the heat until the cheese melts over the potatoes, capping them like snow in the Alps.

10 strips bacon, cut into paper clip–sized pieces
2 tablespoons unsalted butter
2 tablespoons vegetable or olive oil
1 medium onion, chopped
2 garlic cloves, chopped
Dash of balsamic vinegar
3 medium waxy potatoes, peeled and diced
5 eggs
Salt and pepper

Fry the bacon in a 9-inch/23-cm frying pan until crisp. Remove to paper towels to drain. Pour off the excess bacon fat. Add a tablespoon each of the butter and olive oil to the pan. When hot, add the onion and gently sauté until soft and golden. Add the garlic and cook a few minutes more, then remove all to a plate.

Deglaze the pan with the vinegar and reduce until it's almost gone, about 1 minute. Add the remaining tablespoon each butter and olive oil and heat over medium heat. When the fat is hot, add the potatoes and sauté, stirring only very occasionally, until they are soft when pierced with a fork and very crisp and golden on the outside, a good 20 minutes or so. Return the onion, garlic, and bacon to the pan.

Gently beat the eggs together with a fork, season with salt and pepper, and pour over the potatoes. Cook until the eggs appear set on the bottom but are still a bit slithery on top—or, as the French put it, *baveux* ("drool-like"). Cover the omelet and continue cooking until the top sets, no more than a minute or two, because you still want it a bit runny on top. Run a spatula around the edge and slip the omelet out onto a large plate. Serve cut into wedges.

LA CHORIZETTE

[*Serves 4*]

*T*here is a wild little place in Dijon on the rue d'Ahuy that calls itself an *omeletterie-pataterie*. As you might guess, it serves nothing but omelets and potato dishes, but, oddly, the traditional, rustic food stands in contrast to the restaurant itself: crêpe paper streamers in bright yellow, red, turquoise, and green dangle from the ceiling, loud music blasts from behind the bar, pictures and postcards are splashed all over the walls, and the young, energetic, auburn-bobbed raspy-voiced owner, Claudine, teeters on a stool in a corner, leaps up to kiss the regulars, puffs on cigarettes, dances to the songs she knows, flies around with plates of potatoes. . . . This hearty potato and chorizo dish of hers is my favorite on the menu. She piles high absolute Frisbees of it and you can never finish. Well. At least you *say* you'll never finish. . . .

2 pounds/1 kg waxy potatoes
¼ pound/125 g bacon, cut into pieces
1 onion, chopped
1 to 2 tablespoons unsalted butter
1 tablespoon olive oil
½ chorizo sausage (about 5 ounces/150 g), or more if you like, sliced
6 garlic cloves, chopped
1 tablespoon *herbes de Provence*
Salt and pepper
About 1 cup/100 g grated Gruyère cheese

Bring a large pot of water to a boil, and cook the potatoes in it until close to, but not quite, done. Drain, peel, and cut into thick slices.

Fry the bacon in a large sauté pan. Remove to paper towels to drain, leaving about a tablespoon of the cooking fat in the pan. Fry the onion until soft, about 10 minutes, and add to the bacon. Add the butter and olive oil to the pan. Stir in the potatoes and chorizo. Fry until the potatoes are completely tender, about 10 minutes.

Toss in the garlic, herbs, bacon, and onion and cook 2 minutes. Season with salt and pepper. Scatter over the cheese, and cover the pan so that it melts over the potatoes and sausage, about 5 minutes. Serve the *chorizette* piled onto plates with a big leafy salad.

VEGETABLE FLAN

[*Serves 4 as a main course or 8 as a starter*]

The line between what constitutes a starter and what can be a main course is thin for me. Probably this smooth flan (or flans, if you do them in ramekins) would be a first course in France, but I place it in the category of main dishes because it also makes an interesting, attractive supper for nights when I've had it up to the eyeballs with meat. For the record, 2 cups puréed vegetable (choose from: carrot, peas, pumpkin, cauliflower, beet, drained chopped tomato, and so on and on) is about 2 pounds/1 kilogram of vegetables boiled or steamed until soft, drained, and then whizzed in the blender. Be creative with seasonings, using spices rather than herbs if you like, or adding citrus zests (or even a spoonful of juice) depending on the vegetable you've used. The cheese is optional, and changeable. If you don't have stock, you can use all milk. And accompaniments are endless. With pumpkin flan, for example, you could serve toasted pecans, sage, and brown butter; with pea flan, maybe you'd like a mint vinaigrette. With tomato, maybe a green salad with lots of basil leaves in it. The flans are also heavenly plain.

2 cups/500 ml puréed vegetable

1 cup/250 ml chicken stock

1 cup/250 ml whole milk or cream

2 tablespoons grated Parmigiano-Reggiano

Salt and pepper to taste

Pinch of nutmeg

5 eggs, lightly beaten

2 tablespoons chopped fresh herbs, such as parsley, basil, sage, thyme, lemon verbena, marjoram, dill, or rosemary

Preheat the oven to 325°F/160°C. Mix the vegetable with the stock and cream in a saucepan and heat just to the boiling point. Remove from the heat and stir in the cheese and seasonings. Taste. Add more salt and pepper if necessary. Whisk in the eggs. Stir in the herbs.

Pour the mixture into a 4-cup/1-liter baking dish, or divide among eight ½-cup/125-ml ramekins. Set in a larger pan and pour in boiling water to come halfway up the sides of the dish or ramekins. Transfer to the oven and bake until set, 25 to 30 minutes. Let sit for 5 minutes before serving.

NICE AND USEFUL THINGS
TO KNOW ABOUT SOUFFLÉS

The ultimate way to transform leftovers into cloud-nine luxury is to make a soufflé: one big one, individual pots, or flipped out, made-ahead, sauce adorned, pudding-like versions. Everybody loves them, for a starter or main course, and anyone can make them.

The recipe that follows is my basic formula—left loose, because who ever actually makes the same one twice? By puréed vegetable, I mean cooked (boiled or steamed, for example) and then blended or mashed. Choose from: carrot, squash, leek, celeriac, spinach, zucchini, or whatever else you have around; leftovers from Eggplant Tartines (page 9), for example. Instead of a vegetable, you could also use drained canned tuna fish, salmon, or crab. Shredded smoked salmon or haddock, or leftovers from Brandade Peppers (page 115) are also good. Maybe you have leftover ham to chop fine instead. And, if none of these things is on hand, a cheese soufflé is wonderful all on its own: fresh goat's cheese, blue, cheddar, Gruyère, Parmigiano-Reggiano, and so on. For the chopped herbs, there is no end of options either: parsley, tarragon, thyme, dill, rosemary, ad infinitum. Or maybe you're making a mixture that would favor spice, such as curry. Maybe you'll decide just a spoonful of mustard or garlic is enough. The only important thing to remember always is that whatever mixture you create must be seasoned very well, overseasoned in fact, because its taste will be diluted once the egg whites are folded in.

About serving. I'd say a plain soufflé, if it's a good one, should probably be left to speak for itself. But some days I just can't keep my paws off. The simplest thing, then, is to slit their tops at the table and spoon in a bit of sauce. Most pasta sauces are good for this; for example, tomato sauce, thinned-out pesto, blue cheese sauce, lemon sauce, anchovy sauce, and so on. Of course, whatever sauce you choose shouldn't mask the soufflé. The idea is that it should make sense with the flavors in the soufflé and complement them. Pesto sauce in a tomato soufflé, for example, or lemon sauce in a smoked fish soufflé.

Finally there's the famous pudding, or twice-baked, soufflé alternative, the advantage of which is that you can make them early in the day. When you take the soufflés from the oven, let them cool, shrinking back into their ramekins. Then turn them out into 6-inch/15-cm gratin dishes, cover, and set aside. Refrigerate if they are going to be sitting out for more than an hour. Before serving, preheat the oven to 425°F/220°C. Spoon a generous few tablespoons of thin sauce over each soufflé, such as a very light béchamel, or a tomato sauce, or simply some heavy cream with just a grating of nutmeg, salt, and pepper stirred in. Then sprinkle generously with freshly grated Parmigiano-Reggiano and maybe some chopped fresh herbs. Return to the oven until the soufflés have risen up again and are golden on top, with their sauce bubbling gently around them, 5 to 7 minutes. Serve straight out of the oven.

SOUFFLÉ

[*Makes 1 large soufflé to serve 4 as a main course or 8 ramekins, for a first course*]

I, soufflé advocate, have a mouthful of nice (and useful) things to say about them (see pages 74–75).

1 cup/250 ml milk
1 shallot, halved
1 bay leaf
3 tablespoons unsalted butter
5 tablespoons all-purpose flour
3 eggs, separated
1 egg white
1 cup/250 ml puréed vegetable (see page 158)
3 ounces/100 g cheese, grated or mashed
1 generous tablespoon chopped fresh herbs
Pinch of paprika
Salt and pepper

Preheat the oven to 400°F/200°F. Butter a 4-cup/1-liter soufflé dish or eight ½-cup/125-ml ramekins and dust with flour or grated Parmigiano-Reggiano. Bring the milk to a simmer with the shallot and bay leaf in a saucepan. Cover and set aside to infuse for a good 10 minutes.

Melt the butter in another saucepan, whisk in the flour, and cook, still whisking, 1 minute. Strain the milk mixture over it, whisking until smooth, and cook over medium heat until the mixture has thickened and coats the back of a spoon, a matter of a few minutes. Whisk in the egg yolks one at a time. Stir together the vegetable, cheese, herbs, and paprika with a fork. Add to the yolk mixture. Season very generously with salt and pepper. Remove from heat.

Beat the whites into stiff peaks. Stir a spoonful of whites into the vegetable mixture to loosen it, then fold the mixture into the whites. Fill the mold or ramekins, smoothing the tops, and run your finger around the inside edge so that the souf-flé(s) will rise evenly. Set in a roomy baking dish. Pour around boiling water to come two-thirds up the sides. Bake until puffed up and golden on top but still soft, in the center. A large soufflé takes 20 to 25 minutes; the small ones 15 to 25, depending on the filling. Remove from the water and serve immediately.

SEA-SALT SALMON

[*Serves 4*]

I can't tell you what's best about this recipe, the cooking or the eating. Definitely call everyone to watch once you've put the pan on the stove, because as the salt heats, it pops, snaps, crackles, and whispers like a campfire. Then, when you lay the salmon on, its color will rise as it cooks, like blushing cheeks. Because the fish is totally pure with this cooking method, serve some fresh herbs, such as chives or basil, alongside. And you know about crème fraîche if you'd like a dollop of that too.

Coarse sea salt or kosher salt
4 salmon fillets (about ¼ pound/125 g each) with skin
Lemon or lime wedges, optional

Cover the bottom of a large sauté pan with ½ inch/1 cm coarse salt. Set over high heat. Open a window. (I do mean that.)

Lay the salmon fillets on the salt, skin side down. Their color will change from the bottom up as they cook, and they're done the instant the color is even, 15 to 20 minutes, depending on the thickness of the fish.

Peel the salmon from its skin (discarding the skin, which is too salty to eat) and transfer to plates. Serve with a lemon or lime wedge for squeezing. No other seasoning is needed.

CAMEMBERT SALMON

[*Serves 4*]

*Y*ou're thinking, "Ugh, she's got to be kidding." But this is no mental lapse; just because it's strange to the ear doesn't mean it will be on the tongue. The cream mellows out the cheese just enough, still leaving it smooth, thick, and earthy. Salmon's strong personality holds up to that brilliantly. You can serve Camembert Salmon plain or with wilted spinach, or, as I usually do, on a bed of leeks, simply sliced into rings, gently sautéed in butter, and seasoned with salt and pepper (6 leeks are enough for roughly 4 people). If I want to get fancy, I add a step: I finely julienne about 2 extra leeks, then deep-fry them in batches until they're crisp and golden, about 30 seconds. Then I sprinkle on salt. In that case, the plate becomes a field of leeks, with delicate, golden, fried leeks scattered over, the salmon in the center, and the sauce spooned on to each person's liking.

1 small Camembert
½ cup/125 ml cream
2 teaspoons unsalted butter
1 teaspoon vegetable oil
4 salmon fillets (about ¼ pound/125 g each), with skin
Salt and pepper
1 teaspoon cider vinegar, or more to taste

Unwrap the cheese and cut into large pieces. Place with the cream in a saucepan and heat gently, stirring occasionally, to melt. While the cheese melts, heat the butter and oil in a skillet until the skin of the salmon touched to it sizzles immediately. Cook the salmon skin side down until done to your liking.

Meanwhile, season the sauce with salt and pepper. Taste, and add the vinegar. If you'd like it slightly more acidic, add a bit more. Lay a fillet on each serving plate. Spoon around the sauce. Serve immediately.

PARMESAN FLATFISH

[*Serves 4*]

*B*etter than bread crumbs alone, the grated cheese adds a slightly tangy note, freckled with herbs and fluffed around the fillet. It's ready in no time, and good with a squirt of lemon. Serve with steamed snow peas or broccoli on the side.

½ cup/125 ml milk
1 cup freshly grated Parmigiano-Reggiano (3 to 4 ounces/20 g)
¼ cup/20 g fine bread crumbs
1 tablespoon *herbes de Provence*
4 sole, flounder, or other flatfish fillets (about ¼ pound/125 g each)
Salt and pepper
3 to 4 tablespoons unsalted butter

Preheat the oven to broil, with the rack near the top. Pour the milk into a wide bowl. Mix the grated cheese, bread crumbs, and herbs together on a plate.

Dip each fish fillet into the milk to coat, then dip into the cheese mixture to enrobe well. Lay on a greased baking sheet or dish. Sprinkle over any remaining crumb mixture. Season with salt and pepper. Broil until the fish is cooked through and the top is golden and crisp, about 5 minutes.

Meanwhile, heat the butter in a small pan until foaming and turning hazelnut color. When the fish is cooked, remove to plates and drizzle with the foaming brown butter.

BACON COD

*T*his gets high marks for good looks and nice, simple flavors: white fillets belted with a cummerbund of bacon, and pinned with lemon, bay, and thyme. I like bacon cod (or monkfish, or trout) on lentils that have been warmed in a pan with shallots and a bit of balsamic vinegar. But this isn't a competitive dish; it gets along with lots of other accompaniments too.

4 pieces cod fillet (about 5 ounces/150 g each)
Salt and pepper
8 thin lemon slices
8 bay leaves
8 sprigs thyme
8 slices bacon
About 2 tablespoons olive oil

Preheat the oven to 400°F/200°C. Season the fish with salt and pepper. Arrange the lemon slices, bay leaves, and thyme sprigs atop the fillets. Wrap two pieces of bacon around the middle of each, like a cummerbund, to secure the lemon and herbs. Lay the fillets in a baking dish. Drizzle over the olive oil.

Bake until flakingly tender, about 10 minutes. Serve.

PINK AND GREEN PAPILLOTES

[*Serves 4*]

*B*amboo steamers are a regular feature in many urban French kitchens, and after a few months in Paris, worn down by peer pressure, I headed to Chinatown to buy my very own. They looked lovely for months up on the corner shelf in the kitchen, but, no, they never did come down; not, that is, until I met an admirable home cook called Odile. Following a very impressive soufflé at her house one night for dinner, she breezed in with these excellent fish packages as a main course. I was terribly impressed. But, she assured me, they were easy: although the list of ingredients is long, everything just gets thrown together in a little foil pouch and steamed for 15 minutes. She also informed me that my "little-miss" steaming baskets weren't necessary: a vegetable steamer set down in a saucepan with the fish laid in it does just as well.

2 medium cucumbers
1 grapefruit
1 teaspoon mustard seeds
1 teaspoon ground coriander
½ teaspoon cumin
½ teaspoon ginger
½ teaspoon turmeric
4 fish fillets (about 5 ounces/150 g each), such as cod, halibut, or salmon
Salt and pepper
2 garlic cloves, finely chopped
1 spring onion, sliced, including the green tops
4 teaspoons pink peppercorns, lightly crushed
About 2 tablespoons olive oil

Cut four pieces of foil large enough to wrap each piece of fish separately, and set aside. Peel, seed, and very thinly slice the cucumbers lengthwise. Pat dry with a towel and set aside. Peel the grapefruit with a knife, removing all the white pith and exposing the sections. Then cut out the sections, leaving behind the bitter membranes. Set aside 12 sections. Combine the spices in a bowl.

Pat the fish dry with paper towels, season with salt and pepper, and rub generously with the spice mixture. In the center of each piece of foil, arrange a nest of cucumber slices and grapefruit sections. Lay the fish on top. Scatter over the garlic, spring onion, and pink peppercorns. Drizzle lightly with olive oil. Seal the packages and lay in the steamer basket.

Fill a pot with about 2 inches of water. Set the steamer basket in the pot. Cover and steam until the fish is just cooked, about 15 minutes. Transfer the packages to plates and let everyone break in to eat. These need no accompaniment.

ALMOND SOLE

[*Serves 2*]

This classic is one of my favorite ways to eat fish. Steam broccoli or green beans to serve on the side, which takes no time. Then give the fish a sizzling zap for five minutes or so, and eat. Now, the almonds are a fine embellishment, but not necessary. Without them, you get familiar sole meunière, and that's good too. Whichever you make, the recipe calls for clarified butter. To do that, melt about 6 tablespoons butter slowly, then skim off any white froth on the surface. Pour the clear (clarified) butter slowly into a clean bowl, leaving behind the milky sediment at the bottom.

½ cup/**60 g all-purpose flour**
Salt and pepper
½ cup/**60 g clarified butter**
2 skinned, but not deboned, sole (about 7 ounces/200 g each)
½ cup/**125 ml milk**
Half a lemon
½ cup/**30 g slivered almonds, lightly toasted**
A handful of parsley leaves, chopped

Season the flour generously with salt and pepper. Heat the butter in a skillet until it is hot and foaming. Dip the sole first in the milk, then in the flour mixture. Fry immediately in the butter until done, about 3 minutes per side. Remove the fish to a serving plate. Squeeze on lemon juice to taste.

Toss the almonds in the hot butter to warm, add the parsley, and pour over the fish. Serve immediately.

FLOUNDER IN PARSLEY

[*Serves 4*]

*N*ouvelle cuisine was the brunt of many jokes in and after its time, but going back now and looking at recipes from that era, I've found a lot of wisdom. The general idea for this recipe comes from a book published in 1975 called *Revolutionizing French Cooking* by Roy Andries de Groot. I made it because I thought, "What a waste: there's no way that fish is going to get any flavor from the parsley so fast." But the dish proved me wrong. With this cooking method, the flounder emerges perfectly perfumed, and with a texture as delicate as sea scallops.

6 large bunches parsley
½ cup (60 ml) white wine
Salt and pepper
2 flounder fillets (about ⅔ pound/350 g each), skinned and deboned
¼ cup/60 g cold unsalted butter, cut into pieces
2 tablespoons chopped fresh parsley or basil

Preheat the oven to 300°F/150°C. Wash the parsley bunches thoroughly under cold water and shake off the water, leaving what clings to the leaves. Lay half in a baking dish, pour over the wine, and season with salt and pepper. Lay the fish on top and season with salt and pepper. Cover with the remaining damp parsley bunches. Then cover the dish tightly with foil to seal. Bake until the fish is opaque, about 20 minutes.

Remove from the oven and lift off the foil. Strain the juices into a saucepan and bring to a boil. Remove from the heat and whisk in the butter. Season with salt and pepper and stir in the chopped parsley. Set a piece of fish on each of four warm serving plates, discarding the parsley from baking. Pool around the sauce and serve.

CRISP VINAIGRETTE FISH

[*Serves 2*]

*N*ot hungry enough for a first course myself, thought I; I perched my dinner guest on a stool in the corner of the kitchen and turned to the stove to make a starter for him alone. I didn't have a recipe, just ingredients, so it startled me that in less than five minutes I was sliding a plate under his nose that looked terribly appealing. And then, seconds later, that I was moving in on him with a fork. This fish is too good for words, as a starter or as a main course. It's one of those things that you hurl together without thinking, really, which is why this recipe is a little sketchy, full of the dynamism of "live." Try red snapper or any fish fillets that aren't going to flake into bits on you.

2 to 4 red snapper or other fillets (about ¼ pound/125 g per person)
Salt and pepper
3 tablespoons olive oil
About 20 cherry tomatoes, each pierced once with a knife
2 handfuls arugula
1 tablespoon unsalted butter
About 2 teaspoons balsamic vinegar

Season the fish with salt and pepper and set aside. Heat a tablespoon of the olive oil in a skillet and throw in the cherry tomatoes. Toss until hot and splitting, about a minute. Throw the arugula into the pan for just a few seconds to warm. Arrange the tomatoes and arugula on warm plates.

Melt the butter with another tablespoon of the oil in the pan. Fry the fish on both sides until tender and flaky. Transfer to the plates. Deglaze the pan with the vinegar and boil a few seconds to reduce. Pour in the remaining tablespoon of oil and swirl around, then pour it over the fish, arugula, and tomatoes. Grind pepper over, sprinkle with salt, and serve.

French Food at Home

MOUNTAIN DUCK

[*Serves 4*]

*Y*ou're probably picturing some poor lost mallard in hiking boots, yodeling his lungs out in the snowy Alps. Actually, the mountain influence here is cured ham and the duck is just duck, but they get along, all a-slick with the sweet and sour of honey and vinegar. Serve with soft polenta, or smooth mashed potatoes, or Apple Cabbage (page 180), or on a bed of arugula, drizzled with olive oil.

4 boneless duck breasts with skin (about ¾ pound/375 g each)
Salt and pepper
2 small shallots, chopped
2 to 4 tablespoons balsamic vinegar
4 tablespoons honey
2 paper-thin slices prosciutto di Parma, sliced into 1-inch/2.5-cm pieces
2 tablespoons cold unsalted butter

Score crisscrosses into the fat side of the duck with a knife and season well with salt and pepper. Preheat a large skillet, and sauté the breasts fat side down, 5 to 10 minutes. Turn and sear the other side for another 5 minutes, or until done to your liking.

Remove the duck to a carving board to rest. Skim all but 3 to 4 tablespoons of the fat from the pan. Add the shallots and let soften, about 2 minutes. Now add the vinegar and honey. Boil until the sauce is thick and syrupy, about 2 minutes. Meanwhile, heat the prosciutto in a small frying pan until it curls slightly, a minute or two. Remove the sauce from the heat, whisk in the butter, and stir in the ham.

Carve the duck breasts into thin slices and arrange on a serving platter. Pour over the sauce. Serve.

RASPBERRY DUCK

[*Serves 4*]

Nothing this simple should be allowed to be so impressive. The sauce alone fascinates me: bright red with brick-hued swirls and slight hints of orangy electricity where the tomato has met the garlic. It is sweetish, but certainly not too much so, and the acidity of the fresh berries gives it perfect balance anyway. If you don't have raspberry vinegar, be not thwarted, because red wine vinegar works beautifully too.

4 boneless duck breasts with skin (about ¾ pound/375 g each)
Salt and pepper
6 tablespoons raspberry vinegar
2 garlic cloves, crushed
1 heaping tablespoon tomato paste
1 cup/250 ml red wine
2 tablespoons raspberry jam
2 to 3 tablespoons cold unsalted butter
2 to 3 big handfuls fresh raspberries

Score the fat side of the duck breasts with a knife. Season well on both sides with salt and pepper. Heat a large skillet and sauté the breasts until cooked to your liking, for me 7 to 10 minutes on the fat side, then about another 3 minutes on the other. Remove to a carving board to rest.

Deglaze the pan with the vinegar, scraping up the pan juices. Boil to reduce to roughly a tablespoon, about 1 minute. Whisk in the garlic and tomato paste, then whisk in the wine. Boil rapidly to reduce by half, about 5 minutes. Whisk in the jam, then remove from the heat and whisk in the butter, a little at a time, to make a glossy sauce. Strain if you want to get rid of the jam seeds. Season with salt and pepper to taste. Toss in the fresh berries.

Thinly slice the breasts and arrange on a platter, preferably on a bed of arugula. Spoon over the raspberry sauce, and serve.

BEER BIRD

[*Serves 4*]

When I told my poultry man that I wanted a guinea hen to cook in beer, he said, "That's really too bad." But he was wrong. Don't underestimate the value of a can of double malt knocking around in the back of the fridge. Here it bubbles madly around the poultry pieces (chicken is good too) and coats them golden and sticky brown. It licks the garlic into tiny, soft pillows of mellow flavor. It boils down to a dark sauce with smoky undertones of bacon and beady-eyed juniper.

1 guinea hen (about 3 pounds/1.4 kg), cut into 8 pieces
Salt and pepper
2 heads garlic, broken into cloves and peeled
¼ lb/125 g strips bacon, each cut into 4 pieces
6 bay leaves
1 branch rosemary
1 tablespoon juniper berries
2 cups/500 ml beer, preferably double malt

Preheat the oven to 475°F/250°C. Season the hen well with salt and pepper and place in a single layer in a baking dish. Tuck in the garlic, bacon, and herbs. Scatter over the juniper berries. Pour in the beer.

Bake 15 minutes. Turn the pieces over and bake another 15 minutes. Turn again and bake 15 minutes longer. By now the meat should be cooked and sticky with caramelized sauce. If, perchance, the sauce hasn't boiled down quite enough, remove the hen pieces and keep warm, pour the juices into a saucepan, and boil on the stovetop until you've got just enough left for sauce. Pour the sauce over the hen pieces—herbs, juniper, and all—and serve.

CARROT JUICE CHICKEN

[*Serves 4 to 6*]

*T*hree-star chef Alain Passard did this on TV once with a rabbit and I, recalling my late grandfather's homemade carrot juice which I loathed to drink in my youth, thought, "ick." Fortunately, that "ick" was overwhelmed by my fascination with the idea of cooking meat in carrot juice, and so I tried it. Well, what a revelation. Carrot juice added in judicious ladles over browned chicken pieces in a pan cooks down to a caramelized orangey glaze that coats the meat and gives it remarkable taste, flirting with both acidity and sweetness. I still won't *drink* carrot juice, but I'll do this. Try it with rabbit or veal, if you like.

4 chicken legs (about ½ pound/250 g each), split between thigh and drumstick
Salt and pepper
2 tablespoons vegetable oil
1 tablespoon chopped fresh rosemary
1 tablespoon fresh thyme
4 cups/1 l carrot juice

Season the chicken pieces with salt and pepper. Heat the oil in a sauté pan until hot, and brown the chicken pieces well on all sides (working in batches if necessary), a good 20 minutes. Pour all but a tablespoon of fat from the pan and scatter the herbs over the chicken.

Now ladle in about 1 cup/250 ml of the juice and cook until reduced to a syrup. Turn the chicken. Ladle in another ½ cup/125 ml and let it reduce. Continue adding the juice by ½ cups (125 ml), turning the chicken occasionally, until it is tender and coated in a shiny orange glaze. When the last ladle of juice has reduced to a sauce-like syrup, transfer the chicken to a serving platter, drizzle over the pan sauce, and serve.

ORANGE WINGS

[*Serves 4*]

*C*hicken wings are inexpensive, and most of us have an orange or two trailing on the counter. Those ingredients, along with the warmth of cinnamon, the fragrance of coriander, the aromatic base notes of shallot and garlic, and the freshness of mint, make a fairly economical dinner quite eventful.

20 whole chicken wings (about 3 pounds/1.5 kg total)
Salt and pepper
3 tablespoons olive oil
½ teaspoon cinnamon
1 to 2 teaspoons ground coriander
2 shallots, minced
2 garlic cloves, minced
½ cup/125 ml orange juice
Grated zest of 1 orange
¼ cup/125 ml chicken broth
A handful of chopped fresh cilantro or mint

Preheat the oven to 400°F/200°C. Season the wings with salt and pepper. Heat 2 tablespoons of the oil in a large skillet and brown the wings well on all sides, working in batches if necessary. Combine the cinnamon and coriander in a baking dish, then tilt the browned wings into it, tossing to coat. Transfer to the oven and bake until completely cooked, 15 to 20 minutes.

Meanwhile, add the remaining tablespoon of oil to the skillet, and sweat the shallots and garlic until softened, 3 to 5 minutes. Deglaze the pan with the orange juice, scraping up the pan juices. Add the zest. Pour over the broth and boil rapidly to reduce to sauce consistency, 5 to 10 minutes. Taste and adjust the seasonings.

Remove the wings from the oven and toss with the sauce, then with the cilantro or mint. Divide the wings among plates, and pour over any pan sauce that stays behind. Serve with couscous and buttered carrots, or with salad.

TARRAGON CHICKEN

[*Serves 4*]

S ome recipes are a relief. That's how I felt about this one, one night when people I was too tired to have over were coming anyway. It's a bistro dish in its simple execution and appearance, but somehow tarragon, with its refreshing anise scent, raises the whole thing to a higher level.

1 tablespoon unsalted butter
1 tablespoon olive oil
1 chicken (about 3 pounds/1.4 kg), cut into 8 pieces
Salt and pepper
About ¾ cup/175 ml white wine
1 shallot, finely chopped
About 1 cup/250 ml heavy cream
2 to 3 tablespoons chopped fresh tarragon
Lemon juice to taste

Melt the butter with the oil in a large skillet over quite high heat. Season the chicken pieces with salt and pepper and fry in batches until well browned, about 5 minutes per side. Put all the chicken back in the pan, reduce the heat to medium, cover, and cook until tender, about 30 minutes. Remove the chicken to a plate and keep warm.

Deglaze the pan with the wine, scraping up the good bits on the bottom with a wooden spoon. Add the shallot, and boil until the wine has reduced with the cooking juices to make a thickish sauce, about 5 minutes. Add the cream and half the tarragon. Boil down again to thick sauce consistency, 3 to 5 minutes.

Season the sauce with salt and pepper. Squeeze in lemon juice to taste. Put the chicken pieces back in and turn to coat, then transfer to a platter, scraping the sauce over the chicken. Scatter over the remaining tarragon, and serve.

LACQUERED QUAIL

[*Serves 4*]

I almost called this Black Birds, because the sauce really does go dark, jacketing the birds like a wet slicker. You could substitute chicken pieces on the bone here, or probably even pork chops, but I especially appreciate the faint gamy quality of quail against this mysterious, glossy sweet-and-sour coating.

4 quail
4 tablespoons soy sauce
2 tablespoons five-spice powder
2 tablespoons olive oil
3 tablespoons sugar
3 tablespoons honey
2 tablespoons balsamic vinegar

Set the quail in a dish just large enough to hold it. Combine the soy sauce and five-spice powder and pour over. Leave to marinate on the counter for 30 minutes to an hour, turning occasionally.

Heat the oil in a sauté pan with a lid. Brown the birds on all sides. Pour over a cup (250 ml) of water, cover, and braise, turning often, until the meat is tender, about 30 minutes.

Meanwhile, dissolve the sugar and honey in ¼ cup/60 ml water. Uncover the pan and pour it over the birds. Boil, without the lid, to reduce the sauce to a syrupy consistency, turning the birds occasionally to lacquer them in sauce. Add the balsamic vinegar, mixing well. Serve with rice.

HONEY HEN

[*Serves 4 to 6*]

*I*mproved, says a friend of mine, with a jolt of soy sauce and, as he calls Worcestershire sauce, "What's-this-here-sauce." Personally, I just stick to the purely French preparation below, which is exotic enough: chicken pieces cloaked in a gorgeous, deep amber gown of honey, and strewn with herbs from sun-baked Provence. Mind you, I liked the results, too, of rolling the sauce-drenched chicken pieces in sesame seeds before baking, but maybe save that for next time. First try the original with a pyramid of lemony couscous alongside and see how you feel about that.

1 chicken (3 pounds/1.4 kg), cut into 8 pieces
Salt and pepper
½ cup/125 ml honey
2 tablespoons Dijon mustard
1 tablespoon *herbes de Provence*

Preheat the oven to 400°F/200°C. Season the chicken with salt and pepper. Melt the honey in a saucepan and whisk in the mustard and herbs. Pour over the chicken pieces in a baking dish, and roll them around to coat well.

Bake, turning occasionally, until the meat is cooked through, well browned, and veiled in its dripping hot sauce, 40 to 45 minutes.

French Food at Home

SPICE BIRD

[*Serves 4 to 6*]

*S*pice-encrusted chicken is the kind of thing you want to pick up with your fingers and gnaw at outdoors in a shady spot. At the table, however, upright and armed with utensils and good manners, you need a little something on the side. My favorite is diced cucumber, just held together with plain yogurt and seasoned with salt and pepper. If you prefer a smoother partner, try avocado well mooshed up with lime juice, salt, and pepper. Straying from what's below is, as usual, worth trying. So, be free with your spice pickings, not forgetting (another time) the lovely combination of cumin and crushed coriander seeds. But, also be cautious. The chili I buy in France, for instance, makes fire in the mouth; that's why I use only a teaspoon. If your variety is milder, you can always add extra, then, if it still isn't hot enough, add more cayenne pepper. The only way to tell if you've got the spice as you like is to taste the crumb mixture and see.

1 chicken (3 pounds/1.4 kg), cut into 8 pieces
Salt and pepper
½ cup/50 g fine bread crumbs
1 tablespoon paprika
1 teaspoon chili powder
2 teaspoons dried oregano or *herbes de Provence*
Pinch of cayenne pepper
¼ cup/60 ml olive oil, more if necessary

Preheat the oven to broil. Season the chicken with salt and pepper. Combine the bread crumbs with the herbs and spices. Taste, and adjust the amounts if necessary. Coat the chicken pieces with the olive oil, then roll in the spice mixture. Arrange in a baking dish. Pour over any oil left behind.

Broil the chicken for a good 10 minutes. Lower the oven temperature to 350°F/175°C, turn the meat, and drizzle over a little more olive oil if it looks dry. Continue cooking until tender, 20 to 25 minutes longer. Serve warm, or eat cold at a picnic.

GINGER TOMATO MEDALLIONS

[*Serves 4*]

*N*ot a hint of stodgy, beefy monotony here, with the fresh gingery tomato sauce, enlivened with cilantro, piled onto sizzling beef medallions. If you happen not to be a meat eater, make the sauce instead for grilled sea bass, or a like fish. Zucchini Fondue (page 185) accompanies these nicely.

4 beef medallions (about ¼ pound/125 g each)
Salt and pepper
Sugar
2 tablespoons unsalted butter
2 tablespoons olive oil
2 shallots, minced
2 cups chopped seeded tomatoes
2 garlic cloves, minced
1-inch/2.5-cm piece fresh ginger, peeled and minced
Grated zest of 1 lime, plus (optional) a squirt of juice
A handful of chopped fresh cilantro

Season the beef on both sides with salt, pepper, and sugar. Heat the butter and half the oil in a skillet until quite hot. Fry the beef 2 to 3 minutes per side, or to your liking. Remove, wrap in foil, and keep warm.

Add the remaining oil to the pan and soften the shallots, about 2 minutes. Add the tomatoes, with the garlic and ginger, and cook, stirring, about 5 minutes, to warm through and soften slightly. Season with salt and pepper. Add the lime zest and cook another 2 minutes or so. Stir in the chopped cilantro, check the seasonings, and add a squirt of lime juice if it needs more acidity. Pile the tomatoes onto the medallions, and serve.

PICKLE CHOPS

[*Serves 4*]

*C*ornichons, I usually forget, can go into things, not just be served alongside. This dish is the result of my emptying the fridge of its knicky-knacky jars one night, and it's now a house staple. A perfect accompaniment is a haystack of buttery parsleyed noodles.

2 teaspoons unsalted butter
2 teaspoons vegetable oil
2 shallots, chopped
4 pork chops (roughly ⅓ lb/165 g each)
Salt and pepper
¼ cup/60 ml crème fraîche or sour cream
3 tablespoons grainy Dijon mustard
¼ cup/30 g sliced cornichons

Heat half the butter and oil in a sauté pan and cook the shallots until soft. Slide them out and reserve. Season the chops with salt and pepper on both sides. Heat the remaining butter and oil in the same pan until hot, and fry the chops until done, about 5 minutes per side. Remove to a serving plate and keep warm.

Return the shallots to the pan, along with the cream, mustard, and cornichons. Stir for a minute or two to warm through, or boil to reduce if it's a bit thin. Spoon over the chops and serve.

WALNUT VEAL

For those with a more cooperative mortar and pestle than mine, the traditional method is below. But I'll tell you what I really do: put the walnuts in a bag with the peeled garlic cloves, get a meat tenderizer or a hammer, and bang like mad. Then I put the resulting paste into a respectable bowl and carry on, adding the oil and so on. Cheating, possibly, but I redeem myself by buying good walnuts in the shell and cracking them myself; it takes only five minutes and the flavor is incontestably superior. In summer, serve walnut veal (or walnut beef) on a bed of arugula drizzled with olive oil. In cooler seasons, try it with smooth herb-mashed potatoes. Any leftover sauce, incidentally, is nice tossed with pasta. Come to think of it, I'd probably even spread the sauce on toasted French bread, decorate with a leaf of parsley, and serve with drinks.

4 veal cutlets (about ¼ pound/125 g each), pounded
Salt and pepper
1 to 2 garlic cloves, peeled
1 scant cup/80 g walnut halves
¼ cup/60 ml walnut oil
A generous handful of finely chopped, fresh parsley, with some leaves reserved
   for garnish
2 tablespoons drained capers
1 tablespoon unsalted butter
1 tablespoon olive oil

Season the veal with salt and pepper. Cut it into finger-width strips, and set aside. Pound the garlic cloves in a mortar and pestle with the walnuts to make a fine-grained paste, adding a few drops of ice water if necessary to ease the task.

Whisk in the walnut oil until thick and reasonably smooth. Season with salt and pepper. Stir in the chopped parsley and capers.

Heat the butter in a skillet until it turns a hazelnut color. Add the olive oil and let get quite hot. Fry the veal strips until nicely browned and cooked through, about 2 minutes. Heap the veal strips on plates and top each with a dollop of sauce. Garnish with a leaf of parsley, and serve.

BASIL BEEF

This recipe comes from a cookbook geared to men called *Les Jules aux Fourneaux*, which I once optimistically gave to a roommate. As far as I know, this marinated beef was the only thing in it he ever made, but what a find! Thin flags of tender meat bathed in basil and fruity olive oil. It's surprisingly light, not remotely anything you'd ever expect from beef, and the leftovers only improve. Now, don't be alarmed by the raw look of it all at the marinating stage. The meat continues to cook in the lemon juice and in a few hours it *looks* cooked too (I'm talking the color of reasonably well done). I serve peeled whole small boiled or steamed potatoes tossed in olive oil, coarse salt, and cracked pepper on the side.

2 pounds/1 kg beef fillet or boneless rump roast, at room temperature
1 cup/250 ml very good olive oil
Grated zest of 1 lemon
Juice of 2 lemons
1 large bunch basil, chopped
Coarse sea or kosher salt and pepper

Preheat the oven to 375°F/180°C. Roast the meat about 15 minutes. Remove and cool completely.

Slice the beef into very thin slices with a sharp knife. Mix together the oil, lemon zest, juice, and basil. Toss with the meat. Season with coarse salt and pepper.

Spread the mixture in a flat dish, so that the meat is completely submerged in the marinade. Cover, and refrigerate all day or overnight, turning once at half-time. Serve at room temperature.

RHUBARB CHOPS

[*Serves 4*]

The arguments I have had about this dish! If you don't like rhubarb, there's obviously no point trying it, and I'm not going to talk you into it. But if you *do* like rhubarb, here is an interesting way to serve it. The result is golden chops with a mild fruit purée (which is a change from Anglo applesauce), and on a quiet, spring weeknight, the dish provides an unsensational, but good, soothing, and undemanding supper. I was first served it by my Australian friend, Kerry Gardner, on one of her trips to France. Since then, however, I've discovered that the late Edouard de Pomiane includes a version in his hilarious book *Cooking with Pomiane*. This recipe is based on his.

2 pounds/1 kg rhubarb, trimmed and cut into 2-inch/5-cm pieces
3 tablespoons unsalted butter
4 to 5 teaspoons brown sugar
1 teaspoon olive oil
4 pork chops (about ⅓ pound/165 g each)
Salt and pepper

Blanch the rhubarb in a pot of boiling water until limp, about 10 minutes. Drain and rinse in cold water. Melt 2 tablespoons of the butter in a saucepan, add the sugar and stir to dissolve, and stir in the rhubarb. Cook until tender, about 10 minutes.

Heat the remaining tablespoon of butter and the oil in a large skillet until spitting hot. Season the pork chops and fry on both sides until very well browned, about 10 minutes. Remove and keep warm. Pour the rhubarb into the skillet and reheat, stirring to mix with the pan juices. Serve the chops and rhubarb together.

A GOOD COFFEE CHOP

[*Serves 2*]

Using sugar like salt is a trick I recently learned for cooking meat. You simply sprinkle on a pinch with the salt and pepper, and it makes for the most beautifully browned and juicy chop you've ever tasted. There's another "pinch" in this recipe: a small glass of strongly brewed coffee to deglaze the pan and give the cooking juices a detectable, but not easily definable, richness.

1 tablespoon olive oil
1 tablespoon unsalted butter
2 pork chops (about ⅓ pound/165 g each)
Salt and pepper
Sugar
¼ cup/60 ml strong black coffee

Heat the oil and butter in a sauté pan. Season the chops on both sides with salt, pepper, and sugar. Fry on both sides until cooked through and nicely caramelized, about 10 minutes. Remove the chops to warm serving plates.

Add the coffee to the pan and shake to deglaze. Boil to reduce to a thin, syrupy sauce, 1 to 2 minutes. Season with salt and pepper, nap over the chops, and serve.

WINE SAUSAGES

*D*are I say that the wine lightens the sausages? It's the acidity, I suppose, that makes them, at least in the imagination, lose some of their traditional stoutness. I'm a great fan of this preparation, but you have to buy respectable sausages for the results to impress you. If you're stumped for a vegetable, Jerusalem Artichokes with Walnut and Dill (page 182) is an idea.

3 tablespoons unsalted butter
8 thin or 4 fat pork sausages
2 onions, chopped
2 shallots, chopped
1 tablespoon all-purpose flour
1½ cups/375 ml white wine
A handful of chopped fresh parsley

Melt the butter in a large skillet. Prick the sausages with a fork to prevent them from bursting, and brown them on all sides. Remove. Add the onions and shallots to the pan and cook until soft, about 10 minutes. Sprinkle the flour over and stir for 1 minute to combine thoroughly. Whisk in the wine. Return the sausages to the pan, cover, and cook until they are done, about 15 minutes.

Remove the sausages and boil down the sauce if it's too liquid, which is unlikely. Spoon the sauce over the sausages and sprinkle with the parsley to serve.

PEAR PORK

[*Serves 4*]

*E*specially in autumn this dish becomes desirable, when the crunch of leaves is underfoot and your breath puffs out in frosty clouds before your face. Pork chops work here too, if you want a cheaper cut of meat, and browned to amber they look just as lovely with the gilt-shouldered pears and the evergreen sprigs of rosemary tucked in. Serve with chopped endives cooked in butter (see headnote, page 173), Onion Tarts (page 56), or perhaps with caramelized parsnips.

2 pork tenderloins (about ¾ pound/375 g each)
Salt and pepper
3 tablespoons olive oil
¼ pound/125 g bacon, diced
2 large pears, firm and ripe, of any variety, halved, cored, and thinly sliced
4 garlic cloves, peeled and sliced
1-inch/2.5-cm piece fresh ginger, peeled and minced
2 branches rosemary, cut into pieces
¼ cup/60 ml white wine or apple juice
¼ cup/60 ml meat stock

Preheat the oven to 325°F/160°C. Cut the tenderloins in half to make 4 equal logs. Fold under the tapering ends a bit and tie with string to secure, so you have 4 even pieces. Season with salt and pepper.

Preheat a skillet until quite hot. Add 1 tablespoon of the olive oil and fry the bacon dice until cooked, about 2 minutes. Remove, leaving the fat behind, and toss together with the pears, garlic, ginger, rosemary, and another tablespoon of oil in a baking dish. Add the remaining oil to the skillet, if needed. When sizzling, brown the pork well on all sides, about 10 minutes total. Remove and nestle in the baking dish.

Deglaze the skillet with the wine, scraping up the good bits on the bottom, and boil until only about 1 tablespoon remains. Add the stock and boil to reduce to 3 to 4 tablespoons. Pour over the meat. Transfer to the oven and roast until the pears and garlic are soft and the meat cooked through, about 30 minutes.

HERB LAMB

[*Serves 4*]

*J*ust the right amount of savory, crunchy crust on a good lamb chop is hard to beat. This simple herb-based mix enhances the flavors of the meat without overwhelming. Another time, for something more pungent, try green or black tapenade mixed with some bread crumbs as the topping. Or, if mellow's your mood, simply sear the chops plain in oil and butter, and serve alongside polenta, with the sauce from Filo Fish in Red Wine Sauce (page 123) drizzled wantonly about.

8 lamb rib chops
Salt and pepper
2 to 3 tablespoons olive oil, more if needed
4 tablespoons fine bread crumbs
1 heaping tablespoon chopped fresh parsley
1 tablespoon mixed dried herbs, such as thyme and rosemary
1 tablespoon Dijon mustard

Preheat the oven to 450°F/230°C. Season the lamb with salt and pepper and rub with a bit of the olive oil. Heat about a tablespoon of the oil in a sauté pan until quite hot, and sear the meat to brown it, about 1 minute per side. Remove to a baking sheet.

Combine the bread crumbs, parsley, and dried herbs in a bowl. Stir in the mustard and enough of the remaining olive oil (more if needed) to bind. Pack the mixture on top of the chops. Transfer to the oven and roast until the top is crisp and the meat done to your liking, for me, about 8 minutes. Let the meat rest on a carving board for about 10 minutes before serving.

DINNER SLIGHTLY SLOWER

*T*here are times when the last thing I want is food that goes fast. On storming winter afternoons with fierce winds slapping against the house, I make for the kitchen and wait out the rage perched over a pot. In summer, long and restless days awaken other urges, and launching into Brandade Peppers is never more satisfying than it is then. Any time of year, guests are my best excuse for spending hours in the kitchen, and then I don't even want to hear the word "rush." Even in those tired moods when I have energy for sweet nothing, slow dishes can be the most hands-off: Anchovy Beef or Slow Lamb look after themselves in the oven while I plunge into a novel.

I bring this same pace to the table too. When dishes are traditional or have taken special effort to prepare, we're more aware of what eating is meant to be. People linger at the table. They'll pour another glass of wine, keep on talking—and there goes the day. What better way to spend it?

There's something a little old-fashioned in this approach, and in many of this chapter's recipes, but, for me, that's much of the attraction. I like the oblivious indifference to the modern world of, say, Potato Torte or Goose-Fat Duck. I also appreciate it when an ancient recipe shows me that it defies time, and Buckwheat Galettes, minimalist and sleek, do that. There are new dishes in this chapter too: Fish Bowls and Mon Petit Chou are two favorites, and they're examples of what can happen when you work happily and unhurried in the kitchen on a free day. So, never mind the clock; let yourself go.

A NOTE ON STOCKS

*D*etailed and exact recipes for stocks can be found in a number of worthwhile cookbooks. However, not being a detail-friendly and exacting sort of person, I've never followed one. I work from the principles. All stocks, be they fish, chicken, veal, or beef, have this in common: bones are covered with cold water in a pot, to which has been added a small, but proportionate, quantity of aromatics: chopped onion, chopped leek, chopped carrot, bay leaf, thyme sprig, parsley sprigs, and a few peppercorns. No salt. All are simmered (not boiled) uncovered, and skimmed of their surface foam, then strained at the end. Once they're cooled, and the fat has surfaced, it is skimmed off as well.

How the stocks I make differ from one another is not very complicated. Take chicken stock, which is the one I use most often. Mine almost always gets made from the carcass of last night's roast chicken. On the rare occasions when I need stock but am bereft of roasted remains, I buy inexpensive poultry parts, such as wings, or I ask the butcher for backs and necks. The simmering time either way is 1½ hours.

Beef or veal stock is different in an interesting way: The bones get roasted for a good 30 minutes at 450°F/230°C to bring out their full flavor and to give them a rich brown color. The vegetables (in this case, a couple of tomatoes are included) are added to the roasting pan for an additional 20 minutes. Then the whole lot is emptied into a stockpot, the herbs and peppercorns added, the pot filled with cold water, and everything is simmered for 4 to 5 hours.

Fish stock's simmering time is only 30 minutes. Longer won't improve it but will make it bitter. I use fish heads as well as bones, because they contain powerful flavor. I sauté the onion in a little butter in the stockpot before adding the remaining staple stock vegetables, and flavorings, and then the fish bits, which I've taken care to rinse well beforehand. White wine usually ends up in my fish stock too; a cup or so improves it.

SAVORY CARROT CAKE

[*Serves 4 as a light main course or 6 as a starter*]

"*D*elicious," I know, is a word to be used judiciously, but here I must suc-cumb. The flavors are outstanding and no matter how often I make this, I'm always amazed that a bunch of carrots and some mushrooms can produce such results: the consistency is moist, the taste intense, the color appealing, and the feel light. The inspiration for this dish comes from French chef Michel Guérard, whose recipe I've reworked. Serve it as a main course, with sautéed zuc-chini or spinach, or as a starter on a salad of flat parsley leaves, all a-dribble with the orange vinaigrette of Orange Asparagus (page 29).

2 tablespoons unsalted butter or olive oil
1 pound/500 g carrots, peeled and sliced
1 cup/250 ml chicken or vegetable stock
Salt and pepper
1 shallot, chopped
¼ pound/125 g button mushrooms, diced
1 garlic clove, chopped
2 eggs, lightly beaten
1 ounce/30 g Gruyère or Parmigiano-Reggiano cheese, finely grated
2 handfuls finely chopped fresh basil, chervil, or parsley

Melt half the butter in a wide saucepan and sauté the carrots gently until lightly golden, 5 to 7 minutes. Pour over the stock. Season with salt and pepper (no salt if you've used stock made from a cube). Cover the pan and cook over medium heat until the carrots are tender, about 15 minutes. Uncover the pan and con-tinue cooking until the stock has evaporated completely, about 10 minutes more.

While the carrots cook, heat the remaining butter in a small frying pan and soften the shallot, about 3 minutes. Add the mushrooms and continue cooking until soft, about 5 minutes more. Add the garlic and cook 2 minutes.

Preheat the oven to 450°F/220°C. Line a 4-cup terrine or loaf pan with waxed paper. Purée the carrots with a blender until smooth. Whisk the egg into the carrot mixture, then stir in the mushrooms, grated cheese, and chopped herbs. Taste, and adjust the seasonings.

Pour the mixture into the mold. Cover with a lid (or foil) and set in a baking dish. Pour around boiling water to come as far up the sides as possible. Bake until a knife inserted in the center comes out clean, about 40 minutes. Remove the dish from the water bath and let cool 5 minutes before turning onto a serving platter. Serve warm, in slices.

BUCKWHEAT GALETTES

[*Makes about twenty-five 6-inch/15-cm galettes*]

These earthy Breton pancakes are traditionally sheet thin and as big as a bathmat, but I make saucer-sized ones since I own only a crêpe pan to do them in. Now, it's tempting to eat them as they come off the heat, drizzled with melted butter, rolled up, and poked down the hatch. But that way, (a) you don't sit down (and I'm a firm believer in sitting down to eat), and (b) you don't get toppings, like stewed tomatoes and grated cheese, or creamed spinach, or soft hot mushrooms, or warm ratatouille to roll up in them. Alternatively, if you hold out for a whole stack of galettes, you can roll in them any of those things, pour over béchamel or tomato sauce, sprinkle with cheese, and *gratiner* the lot. Make some extra to freeze for a quick dinner later in the week. And, if you have leftovers trailing, brush them with butter, drape them like upside-down baskets over metal molds, and toast them in the oven until they are crisp and hold their shape, about 5 minutes. Fill these cups with creamy fish salad, for example, and serve as a starter.

1 cup/125 g buckwheat flour
1 cup/125 g whole wheat or all-purpose flour
½ teaspoon salt
3 eggs, lightly beaten
1 cup/250 ml milk, preferably buttermilk
2 tablespoons vegetable oil
About 2 tablespoons clarified butter, or more vegetable oil, for frying

Sift the flours together with the salt into a bowl. Whisk in the eggs, milk, and oil to achieve a smooth batter. Cover and leave to sit at room temperature for at least 2 hours (refrigerate if longer). Before frying, stir in enough water to bring the batter to the consistency of thin cream.

Melt the clarified butter in a frying pan until medium hot. Pour about 2 table-spoons of batter into the pan and swirl it around to cover the bottom thinly. Fry the galette until the edges crisp and curl and the underside is golden, about 3 minutes. Flip and continue cooking to finish, about another 2 minutes. Continue to make galettes until you've used all the batter; as you cook, pile the pancakes onto a plate, to keep warm in the oven. Serve warm, with the garnish of your choice.

POTATO TORTE

[*Serves 6 to 8*]

*T*his recipe comes from the Auvergne, smack-central France, a region whose haunting, rugged wildness I find magnetic. The food of the place is appropriately simple and hearty: lots of sausages, cabbage, blue cheeses, walnuts, and potatoes. But sometimes simple can be grand. For instance, this impressive favorite of mine, *pâté de pommes de terre*, is decadent and rustic all at once. Plus it comes with a secret, and I'm always a sucker for those: prepare the ingredients a day early so that the potatoes slice neatly and the cream has time to infuse with garlic and herbs—that small step makes all the difference.

3 pounds/1.5 kg waxy potatoes
3 cups/750 ml crème fraîche
1 head garlic, broken into cloves, peeled, and minced
1 large bunch parsley, chopped fine
Salt and pepper
About 1 pound/500 g ready-made puff pastry (2 sheets)
1 egg, lightly beaten

A day before making the dish, boil the potatoes whole in their skins until tender. Rinse under cold water, and set aside to cool completely, then cover and refrigerate. Stir together the crème fraîche, garlic, and parsley. Season generously with salt and pepper. Cover and refrigerate overnight.

About an hour before eating, preheat the oven to 400°F/200°C. Slice the potatoes into neat ¼-inch/5-mm rounds. Roll one sheet of the pastry into an 11-inch/28-cm circle and lay it on a greased baking sheet. Leaving a 1-inch/2.5-cm margin all around, cover it with an overlapping layer of potato slices. Season with salt and pepper. Spread over a layer of the cream mixture. Repeat the layering, tapering in a bit as you go, until all the potatoes and cream have been used and the end result looks like an upside-down double-crusted pie. Usually I have three layers each of potato and cream.

Roll the second pastry sheet into a 12-inch/30-cm circle. Brush the margin of the bottom pastry with the egg and drape the larger round over. Line up the edges and roll the under pastry margin up over the top one to seal, scalloping as you go all the way around. Brush the torte all over with the egg and decorate the surface with the tines of a fork, if you like. Cut an opening about the size of a quarter in the top to let the steam escape during baking.

Bake 10 minutes. Reduce the oven temperature to 375°F/190°C and continue baking until hot through and the pastry is well browned, about 25 minutes. If the torte starts browning too quickly, lay a piece of foil loosely on top. Remove from the oven, and slide onto a large plate for serving. Cut into wedges, and serve with green salad.

BRANDADE PEPPERS

[*Serves 4 as a main course or 8 as a starter*]

So you have to soak the cod and that scares you off. Don't let it. It's no more difficult than watering someone's plant for the weekend. And it's surprising, in fact, how quickly you start to get into this sort of nurturing activity: filling an ice-cold bath for the fish, coming by later and giving a poke, changing the water, feeling the texture of the flesh transform, giving it a rinse. Besides, I always feel smug striding home with an oversized boomerang of salt-stiffened fish in my grip, confident that I actually know what to do with it. You can serve brandade in a small flat dish, gratinéed and eaten with toast. But in a slippery hot red pepper pouch, drizzled with a bit of vinaigrette, it's even better. Leftovers can be made into fish cakes or used for soufflé.

2 pounds/1 kg salt cod
2 to 4 garlic cloves, crushed
1 pound/500 g starchy potatoes
8 red peppers
1 cup/250 ml milk
½ cup/125 ml olive oil

Cut the cod into pieces and soak for 2 days in cold water, changing the water often. Drain.

Preheat the oven to broil and set the rack near the top. Put the fish in a pot of fresh cold water, and bring slowly to a boil. Remove from the heat when the water bubbles. The fish should be tender. Drain and cool. Remove any bones and mash with a fork, adding the garlic as you do so. Cook the potatoes whole in a pot of boiling water until tender. Drain, peel, and mash.

While the potatoes cook, broil the peppers on a baking sheet, turning occasionally, until their skins are black and cracking, 15 to 25 minutes. Remove to a bowl. Cover with plastic wrap and let sit a few minutes to steam. Skin the peppers and cut off the tops, like pumpkins, to remove the seeds. In an ideal world, you'd now have 8 whole pepper pockets. In real life they rip, but this is not a problem, because they'll patch up cooperatively later.

Scald the milk in one saucepan. Heat the oil in another. Stir the hot oil into the fish, adding it slowly. Now stir in the mashed potatoes, adding them alternately with the milk, until you have a smooth purée. Season with salt and pepper. Stuff the peppers with the purée, or patch them up to make it look as though you have. Set in a baking dish and reheat before serving. Serve with green salad drizzled with a balsamic vinaigrette.

FISH BOWLS

I'm so pleased with this recipe I could burst. It's not a soup, per se, but poached pieces of fish, surrounded with colorful, finely cut vegetables, all bathed in a pool of warm, frothy, barely curry-scented broth. It takes a bit of time and attention, but who cares, because every bite is a gift to the tongue. Another advantage of this gently flavored bowl is that it is light, so with it as a main course flanked by a starter and dessert, you'll rise from the table like a feather. Apart from cooking the fish, almost everything here can be prepared reasonably far in advance.

FOR THE COURT BOUILLON

1 carrot, diced
1 onion, diced
White of 1 leek, diced and rinsed
6 black peppercorns
1 bay leaf
1 parsley sprig
1 cup/250 ml white wine
4 cups/1 l cold water

FOR THE BOWLS

1 medium yellow pepper, diced
1 carrot, diced
White of 1 leek, cut into fine julienne and rinsed
6 pieces halibut fillet (about ¼ pound/125 g each), skinned
6 small handfuls arugula
2 tablespoons drained capers
Salt and pepper

TO FINISH

2 tablespoons cold unsalted butter, cut into pieces
½ teaspoon curry powder
Salt and pepper

To make the court bouillon, put all the ingredients in a heavy saucepan, bring to a boil, and simmer 30 minutes. Strain into a sauté pan that will be large enough to accommodate the fish.

Bring the liquid to a boil and add the yellow pepper, carrot, and leek. Cook until tender, 5 to 7 minutes. Remove with a slotted spoon and rinse under ice-cold water to preserve their color. Set aside.

Reduce the heat of the poaching liquid to a simmer and lay in the fish. Poach until just cooked, 5 to 7 minutes. While the fish cooks, lay out six warmed soup plates. Divide the arugula, capers, and cooked vegetables among them. Season with salt and pepper.

When the fish is cooked, remove with a slotted spoon, and lay a piece in each bowl. Strain 2 cups/500 ml of the poaching liquid into a saucepan and quickly bring to a boil. Remove from the heat and whisk in the butter, one piece at a time, or use an immersion blender. Whisk in the curry powder. Season with salt and pepper. Taste, and adjust the seasonings. Ladle over the fish, and serve immediately.

TIED FISH

[*Serves 4*]

*F*ish stuffed and tied with string is appealingly rustic. And, here, it's another case of habitual ingredients seeming, all of a sudden, unusually tasty. You cook equal amounts of diced staple vegetables until soft and golden, then splash over white wine that boils away leaving them sticky, stir through coral-colored shrimp and a scattering of thyme, then sandwich the mixture between fish fillets with skin seared crackling crisp. Or at least that's one way to go about it. I also apply the concept to individual portion-sized fish such as whiting or trout. And, I've had good luck with other stuffings, too, such as ratatouille. With my favorite version here, a sautéed, green, leafy vegetable is the right accompaniment for taste and appearance.

2 tablespoons butter
1 onion, finely diced
White of 1 leek, finely chopped and rinsed
1 celery rib, finely diced
1 to 2 carrots, finely diced
1 bass, red snapper, or halibut (about 3 pounds/1.4 kg), cleaned
½ cup/125 ml white wine
Salt and pepper
20 small cooked shrimp (about 7 ounces/200 g), peeled and chopped
A handful of chopped fresh thyme leaves
2 tablespoons vegetable oil

Melt the butter in a sauté pan. Add the onion, leek, celery, and carrots and cook until soft and starting to caramelize, 25 to 30 minutes. Meanwhile, remove the fillets from either side of the fish by first cutting down the backbone and then working from head to tail. I always leave the tail attached to one of the fillets because I like the look of it. Discard the head and bones, or save them for making stock. All of this, of course, you can have done by the fishmonger.

Preheat the oven to 425°F/220°C with a baking sheet on the rack (the hot sheet will ensure that the skin stays crisp). When the vegetables are ready, pour over the wine and continue cooking until it has evaporated completely and the vegetables are sticky, 5 to 7 minutes. Season with salt and pepper. Remove from the heat, stir through the shrimp and thyme, and set aside.

Heat the oil in a nonstick frying pan (or washed-out sauté pan) large enough to accommodate the fish fillets. When sizzling hot, sear the fillets skin side down just long enough to make the skin crisp, about 3 minutes. Remove.

Take the baking sheet from the oven with oven-mitted hands. Drizzle on a little oil. Lay on the fillet with the tail, skin side down. Top with the vegetable stuffing. Lay on the second fillet, skin side up. Slide three pieces of string underneath at intervals and tie around the fish. Slip the baking sheet back into the oven and bake until the fish is flaky and tender, no more than 10 minutes.

Remove from the oven, slide the fish onto a serving platter, strings and all, and serve.

FENNEL BASS

*F*ish should be served whole more often, natural looking, genuine, and generous. Here there is one whole fish for every two eaters, small bass adorned
with three different anise tastes: caramelized fennel bulb, which creates a base;
feathery fennel herb stuffed into the fish; and, on top, pale pastis-flavored foam
spooned luxuriously over. You might expect the layered flavors to be overwhelming, but the components are delectably mellow and harmonious.

2 bass (about 1 pound/500 g each)
About 1 tablespoon olive oil
Salt and pepper
4 fennel bulbs with plenty of feathery greens
2 tablespoons unsalted butter
2 bay leaves
2 garlic cloves, minced
2 egg yolks
1 tablespoon pastis, Pernod, or other anise-flavored liqueur
½ cup/125 ml white wine
A good handful of chopped fresh parsley

Preheat the oven to broil. Slash the fish about 3 times on each side with a knife.
Rub the skin with the olive oil, and season the fish inside and out with salt and
pepper. Remove the feathery green leaves from the fennel bulbs (or use dill) and
stuff into the fish, reserving a few sprigs for garnish.

Peel, core, and thinly slice the fennel bulbs. Melt the butter in a sauté pan, add
the bay leaves, and heat for 1 minute. Add the sliced fennel and garlic, cover, and
cook gently, stirring occasionally, until soft and caramelized, 20 to 25 minutes.
Season with salt and pepper. Set aside covered, to keep warm.

Broil the fish until cooked through, 5 to 7 minutes per side. Meanwhile, make the
sauce. Whisk the yolks, pastis, and 1 tablespoon of the wine in the top part of a

double boiler. Season with salt and pepper, and set over barely simmering water. While whisking, add the remaining wine, little by little, until the mixture has doubled in volume and become thick and moussey, about 3 minutes. Check the seasonings. If you're not quite ready to serve, you can leave the sauce over the warm water (heat off) for a few minutes.

To serve, divide the sautéed fennel between two small serving platters. Lay a fish on top of each, spoon over the sauce, garnish with a few sprigs of fennel, and serve.

FILO FISH IN RED WINE SAUCE

[*Serves 4*]

A number of classic French dishes testify to the success of fish and red wine together in cooking. This recipe is a more modern take: fish wrapped in light, crisp filo pastry, with a glossy red wine sauce pooled around. And it's not the bother it might sound either. The sauce is basically a matter of boiling, and the fish is slipped into the oven for about ten minutes. Of course, there's always room for improvisation. If you don't have filo pastry, serve crisp potato slices alongside for texture instead. Or, fry the fish with its skin on so that it plays the crisp part, and serve it on herb-flecked mashed or crushed potatoes. The other thing would be to pinch the red wine sauce right out of the recipe one day and have it with grilled beef medallions or lamb chops and polenta.

1½ cups/375 ml red wine
1 shallot, peeled
1 bay leaf
2 to 3 thyme sprigs
1 sprig parsley
4 peppercorns
1 to 2 teaspoons sugar
1 cup/250 ml veal or beef stock
1 to 2 tablespoons cold unsalted butter
Salt and pepper
4 white fish fillets (about ¼ pound/125 g each)
8 sheets filo pastry, defrosted according to package directions
2 tablespoons unsalted butter, melted
2 to 3 teaspoons *herbes de Provence*

Preheat the oven to 400°F/200°C. Start the sauce, either, properly, in a saucepan or, for speed, in a sauté pan: Boil the wine with the shallot, bay leaf, thyme, parsley, peppercorns, and sugar to reduce by half, 10 to 15 minutes. Add the stock and boil to reduce by half again, or until the mixture has reached sauce consistency and coats a spoon, about 10 minutes more. Remove from the heat and whisk in the cold butter, one piece at a time, until glossy. Season with salt and pepper.

While the wine boils, pat the fish dry with a towel. Brush half the filo sheets with the melted butter, then lay one of the remaining sheets on top of each for double thickness. Lay a fish fillet on each, season with salt and pepper, and sprinkle over the herbs. Now wrap the pastry around the fish into packages and set on a baking sheet.

Bake until the fish is cooked and the pastry crisp and golden, 7 to 10 minutes. Remove to warm plates, spoon around the sauce, and serve.

SALMON POACHED IN OLIVE OIL

[*Serves 4*]

*I*t's not that this recipe takes any time to make, but it is luxurious with all the olive oil, even if you do use an inexpensive kind, which I recommend. What's remarkable about the gentle poaching in warm, fragrant oil is that the fish emerges extraordinarily supple, cooked to absolute perfection. The garnish of diced tomato and shredded basil leaves mixed with a bit of the warmed oil and spooned over is all that's needed. Serve the salmon on Green Beans with Shallots and Toasted Almonds (page 174), substituting toasted pine nuts in place of the almonds. Cucumber slices lightly sautéed is another good base. Once the fish is poached, cool the leftover oil, strain it through a fine-mesh sieve, and store it in a jar in the refrigerator for the next time. Halibut and trout are also otherworldly cooked like this, so "next time" should be soon.

4 skinned salmon fillets (¼ pound/125 g each)
Salt and pepper
About 1½ cups/375 ml olive oil, more if needed
1 tomato, seeded and finely diced
8 basil leaves, shredded
1 teaspoon balsamic vinegar

Season the salmon fillets with salt and pepper and lay them in a frying pan or saucepan just large enough to hold them. Pour in oil to just cover them. Heat gently until the oil is quite warm to the touch. Turn off the heat and let the fish sit in the oil to poach until cooked but still pink in the center, 10 to 15 minutes.

When it's cooked, remove the fish to serving plates. Pour all but ¼ cup/60 ml of the oil out of the pan. There will be a bit of fish residue at the bottom, which you want to hang on to for flavor. Add the tomato and basil to the oil, taste, and add salt and pepper if needed. Heat for just a minute, then spoon around the fish, and let fall a few raindrops of vinegar around each. Serve immediately.

TUNA IN FRAGRANT WATER

[*Serves 4*]

When I think tuna, I think raw. But I've learned that that's not the only way to go about it. This simple poaching method, netting the fish with faint hints of fennel seed and orange, cooks the fish so that its flesh collapses, most unfashionably, at the touch of a fork. I serve this, and I'd almost say it's imperative, with Carrot Juice Carrots (page 175), whose stunning sunshine-colored sauce sets off the basil-napped tuna beautifully, and whose flavors complement the orange and fennel here nicely.

2 medium onions, thinly sliced

8 garlic cloves, minced

1 carrot, diced

1 strip orange zest, any white pith removed

1 tablespoon fennel seeds

12 peppercorns

Coarse sea or kosher salt

¼ cup/60 ml olive oil

12 basil leaves, shredded

1 thick slice tuna (about 1½ pounds/750 g)

Put the onions, 3 of the minced garlic cloves, the carrot, orange peel, fennel seeds, peppercorns, and a few pinches of coarse salt into a sauté pan. Pour over 4 cups/ 1 liter cold water. Bring to a boil, turn down to low heat, and simmer 15 minutes.

Meanwhile, put the remaining minced garlic in a saucepan and pour over the olive oil. Heat very gently, without allowing the garlic to color, about 5 minutes. Turn off the heat, swirl in the basil, cover, and set aside to infuse.

Slip the tuna into the liquid in the sauté pan and cook, uncovered, 45 minutes. Lift the tuna from its poaching liquid and transfer to a warm serving platter. Season with salt and pepper and nap with the basil-garlic oil. Serve.

LETTUCE-WRAPPED SEA BREAM

[*Serves 4*]

"*S*imple" is a complicated word, and in his book *Simple French Cooking*, the late Richard Olney spent several pages defining it before presenting recipes like rabbit sausages, frog ravioli, and, most challenging of all to our notions of simple, braised stuffed oxtail ("requiring a couple of hours' preliminary work and, in all, some six hours' attention on the following day, the last two of which should be more or less undivided"). By comparison, Herb-Stuffed Bass in Lettuce Casing, of which my recipe is a close facsimile, is a breeze. What's more, it's one of the most fabulous fish dishes I've ever tasted: that sour note of sorrel, that licorice hint of tarragon, that garlicky cream, that bright lettuce green . . . With one bite, my faith in Richard Olney's tastes, and in his idea of simplicity, was absolute. If you'd rather use one large sea bass instead of the sea bream, the weight should be about 1½ pounds/750 g.

1 large head Boston lettuce
½ pound/250 g spinach
1½ cups/2 ounces/60 g stale bread, crumbled
4 tablespoons unsalted butter, softened, more if necessary
A handful of finely shredded sorrel leaves
A handful of finely chopped fresh parsley
1 teaspoon finely chopped fresh tarragon
1 egg
Salt and pepper
2 sea bream (¾ pound/375 g each), scaled, gutted, and deboned
2 tablespoons finely chopped shallots
A handful of chopped fresh chives
½ cup/125 ml white wine
½ cup/125 g heavy cream

Preheat the oven to 450°F/230°C. Bring a pot of salted water to boil. Separate the lettuce leaves, trim off any hard white parts, and blanch no more than a minute. Remove, rinse under cold water, and lay on tea towels to dry thoroughly. Remove the stems from the spinach and blanch the leaves in the lettuce water until softened. Drain, rinse in ice-cold water, squeeze dry, and chop.

Mash together the spinach, bread crumbs, and half the butter in a bowl with a fork. Add the sorrel, parsley, and tarragon. Mix in the egg. Season with salt and pepper. Stuff the fish with the mixture and season well all over. Now, wrap the stuffed fish from head to tail, like a mummy, in the lettuce leaves.

Sprinkle the shallots and chives in the bottom of a buttered baking dish and lay the fish on top. Pour in the wine. Dab the remaining butter on the fish. Lay a piece of foil or buttered parchment lightly over the fish and bake 30 minutes, basting occasionally with the pan juices for the last 15 minutes.

Remove the fish to a serving dish and set the baking dish with its cooking juices on a low burner. Whisk in the cream and boil to reduce to sauce consistency. Season with salt and pepper. Serve the fish by cutting into cross-sections and spooning over the warm sauce.

THIS IS NOT A RECIPE
FOR ROAST CHICKEN

*A*long with the onslaught of recipes for stocks, mayonnaise, and white bread, "roast chicken" has appeared in the chicified "basics" section of every cookbook imaginable for the past decade. So, why am I . . . ? you ask. The reason is that most of us are still not roasting chickens often enough, and we're missing out. What holds us back, I suspect, is that roast chicken is precisely the kind of food for when we *don't* want to follow a recipe. We've thought to buy the chicken and that's as much mental effort as we can spare to put into it. Nobody wants to face measuring cups, and a meat thermometer, and a list of fussy instructions.

Instead, we shut our tired eyes: we *do* know the roast-a-chicken routine. Put a salt-, pepper-, and butter rubbed bird on its right side in a hot oven (400°F/200°C) and give it about 20 minutes. Turn it on its left side for another 20 minutes. Turn it breast side up and continue roasting, basting fairly obsessively, until a leg pulls loose easily and the juices run clear, about 20 minutes longer.

That's all we ever need to dredge up to get the job done, and beautifully done at that. But, some fortunate evenings, as we pull a chicken from the market bag, the evasive kitchen muse flies furtively past singing creative grace notes into our ears: "parsley, sage, rosemary, and thyme," for instance, "not to mention tarragon and bay leaves." Suddenly, some combination thereof appears in the cavity of the bird, now being trussed. Other times, we're hit with the inspiration to mash a few garlic cloves into the half cup or so of butter to smear over the bird. Perhaps we slice garlic and slide slivers in under the skin with herbs, or maybe we just poke heaps of garlic cloves into the cavity along with those same herbs. If there's a piece of lemon kicking around, we nudge that in there too. And we can always draw on a vast collection of eccentricities passed along to us from other cooks. I was once told, by a very strange Frenchwoman, that peeled bananas crammed into a chicken's cavity with a few handfuls of green grapes makes for a fine dish. Following the advice of someone rather more balanced, I placed 10 whole stars of anise in the cavity and enjoyed one of the best roast chickens in my memory. Five-spice powder blended with crushed coriander seed makes an exotic rub for the skin. Some like a bird wrapped with bacon and stuffed with onions. And I've recently read about mixing homemade garlicky herb croutons, thyme leaves, salt, and pepper with walnut oil to bind, and stuffing chicken with that, which I can't wait to try.

Now, let's not forget other potential roasting-pan partners that might huddle about the chicken in solidarity with it and our appetites. Heads of garlic with their tops lopped off, peeled shallots or onions or leeks, carrots, potatoes, parsnips, turnips, tomatoes, and so on. I dribble whatever it is with a little olive oil, sprinkle with salt and pepper, and leave it at that. Somehow, I never bother with gravy, although I'm grateful when my mother does. Instead, I carve and serve my bird with the pan juices poured lazily over. And the carcass, later, is inevitably destined for stock (see page 108).

CHICKEN IN VINEGAR

[*Serves 4*]

From cookbook author Anne Willan I learned her version of this classic recipe during my stay at her home in Burgundy. To tell the truth, I like it even better than sautéed chicken in wine, because the extra acid and lack of cream makes a tangier, less cloying dish.

1 chicken (3½ pounds/1.6 kg), cut into 8 pieces
Salt and pepper
3 tablespoons unsalted butter
1 head garlic, broken into unpeeled cloves
1 cup/250 ml red wine vinegar
1 pound/500 g tomatoes, roughly chopped
1 tablespoon tomato paste
1 bouquet garni
1 cup/250 ml chicken stock
Chopped fresh parsley

Season the chicken with salt and pepper. Melt 2 tablespoons of the butter in a large sauté pan until foaming, then, a few pieces at a time, brown the chicken well on all sides. You're not cooking the chicken here; just making the skin crisp and giving it color, so 5 minutes per side is about right. Remove the chicken to a plate.

Add the garlic to the pan and cook about 10 minutes. Deglaze the pan with the vinegar and boil to reduce by half, 10 to 15 minutes. Return the chicken to the pan. Add the tomatoes, tomato paste, and bouquet garni. Simmer, uncovered, until the meat falls from the bone, about 30 minutes. Transfer the chicken to a dish, cover, and keep warm.

Pour the stock into the pan juices and boil until thickened, about 10 minutes. Strain into a saucepan, and if it's still not concentrated enough for your liking, boil it down a little more. Whisk in the remaining tablespoon of butter. Season, and pour over the chicken. Serve with chopped parsley sprinkled over, and with a bowl of roasted or mashed potatoes on the side.

HOUSEWIFE CHICKEN

[*Serves 4*]

*I*f ever you find yourself with only one burner in operation, this is your bird. It has all the dignity of an oven-roasted chicken, surrounded with a rich, old-fashioned accompaniment of bacon, mushrooms, onions, and potato, all done in one casserole on the stovetop. The bacon and vegetables of this classic are meant only to be garnish, but I always end up wanting more of them, so I've doubled the quantities. Homey dishes like this one should exude generosity.

1 chicken (3 pounds/1.2 kg)
Salt and pepper
1 head garlic, broken into unpeeled cloves
2 tablespoons unsalted butter, duck fat, or vegetable oil
¼ pound/125 g bacon, diced
18 pearl onions
⅓ pound/165 g button mushrooms, halved if large
1 to 2 tablespoons olive oil
4 medium waxy potatoes, peeled and diced
A generous handful of chopped fresh parsley

Season the bird inside and out with salt and pepper. Stuff with the garlic cloves and truss.

Melt half the butter in a casserole and cook the bacon until crisp and the onions soft, about 15 minutes. Remove and set aside. Cook the mushrooms about 5 minutes. Add to the onions. Add a tablespoon of olive oil to the pot and cook the potato dice until brown, about 25 minutes. Remove and set aside with the other garnishes.

Add the remaining butter and more olive oil if necessary to the casserole, heat until foaming, and brown the chicken well, about 5 minutes per side. Reduce the heat to low, cover the casserole, and cook the chicken, turning occasionally, until almost tender, 45 minutes to an hour.

Put the onions, bacon, mushrooms, and potatoes back in, cover, and continue cooking until the garnish is hot and the chicken completely cooked, about 10 minutes more. Transfer the bird to a serving platter, arranging the garnish around and pouring over any pan juices. Sprinkle over the parsley and serve, carving at the table.

GOOSE-FAT DUCK

[*Serves 8*]

*C*onfit of duck is one of those preparations I always thought "I just don't do." Until I did. Until I sat picking at it, incredulous of its goodness as soon as it was out of the oven, and left nothing to put up for mellowing in jars. It's a fat dish, yes, so don't waste it on anyone who can't let loose and appreciate decadence. Accompany the duck with winter greens or, to be extreme, with heaps of "frites" (page 157). To preserve it, put the duck legs into sterilized jars, pour over the cooled cooking fat to cover, seal, and store in a cool place for a month.

8 duck legs
1 cup/250 g coarse salt
3 peppercorns
3 bay leaves
3 thyme sprigs
2 garlic bulbs, broken into unpeeled cloves
4 cups/1 l goose or duck fat, more if needed

Put the duck legs in a glass bowl with the salt, peppercorns, and herbs. Cover with a tea towel and refrigerate 24 hours (not less than that).

Preheat the oven to 300°F/150°C. Fish the duck and herbs from the salt and rinse. Put them in a baking dish. Tuck in the garlic. Pour over enough fat to cover the duck legs completely. Cover with foil and bake until the meat collapses at the touch of a finger, about 3 hours. Remove from the oven.

Some say the duck should now be cooled, put in jars, covered in the fat, and refrigerated for at least a week so the flavors mellow before moving along to this next step. I've never had the patience myself. So, hike the oven temperature up to broil. Scoop the duck and garlic from the fat. Lay the duck skin side up on a baking sheet. Broil until the skin is golden and very crisp, about 15 minutes. Serve with the garlic cloves.

French Food at Home

HOLIDAY HEN

[*Serves 4*]

*I*t was during the few days between Christmas and New Year when I, beginning to note a sudden snugness of trousers, decided to take a break from all the feasting. As if on cue, my friend Ivan, king of home cooks, and his companion invited me to dinner. So much for my resolve: it was thwarted by an irresistible guinea hen, which Ivan deboned completely, rolled like a Yule log, baked, and then sliced to reveal an outside ring of white meat around a stuffing of dark meat mixed with fried bread crumbs, onion, garlic, and herbs, and, finally, at the center, a ruby string of cranberries. Replace the guinea hen with duck, chicken, or turkey if you prefer, obviously adjusting quantities for the stuffing according to the size of your bird. Or, if you have a crowd, simply make two guinea hens. Serve with a vegetable purée (see page 158), or Lemon Spinach (page 177), and either cooked cranberries or a cranberry chutney.

1 guinea hen (about 3 pounds/1.5 kg)
Salt and pepper
3 tablespoons unsalted butter
3 tablespoons olive oil, plus a little more for rubbing
1 small onion, chopped
½ cup/15 g dried French-bread crumbs
2 garlic cloves, minced
2 tablespoons chopped fresh parsley
About 40 fresh cranberries

Debone the hen completely (see page 137), or have the butcher do it (neatly) for you. Remove the dark meat from the legs and chop very fine, with a knife or in a food processor. Lay the main part of the bird flat, skin side down. There will be a rough rectangle of skin with the two breasts, with their two smaller fillets attached, on top. Remove one small fillet and lay between the breasts to fill the indentation. Use the other to fill any gaps. Push and prod the white meat, butterflying where necessary, to make an even square of white meat roughly centered on the skin, about 6 inches/15 cm square and about 1 inch/2.5 cm thick. Season with salt and pepper.

Heat 1 tablespoon each of the butter and oil in a frying pan. Sauté the onion until soft but not brown, about 10 minutes. Remove to a bowl. Melt a second tablespoon each of butter and oil in the same pan, and fry the bread crumbs until golden and crisp, 3 to 5 minutes. Mix the crumbs with the onions, adding the garlic and parsley. Now add the minced meat from the legs and combine thoroughly. Season with salt and pepper.

Preheat the oven to 325°F/160°C. Spread the stuffing evenly over the white meat, leaving a bit of a margin around the edges. Make an indentation down the center and fill with a line of cranberries, 2 to 3 cranberries wide. Cover with the stuffing. Now, roll up the meat and tuck in the ends to make a rough log. You may want to trim a bit of skin here and there. Rub the log with a little olive oil. Wrap in foil and secure the ends. Roll once or twice on the counter to make the log perfectly shaped. Wrap in a second layer of foil. (If you've prepared the bird in advance, refrigerate until about 3 hours before cooking.)

Lay the foil log in a baking dish. Bake until completely cooked through but still moist, about 3 hours. Peel off the foil. Heat the remaining 1 tablespoon each butter and oil in a skillet and brown the log on all sides. (Alternatively, remove the skin first.) Trim the ends of the log, and cut into neat slices about 1½ inches/4 cm thick.

HOW TO DEBONE A BIRD

1. Lay the bird breast side down on a cutting board.

2. Run a knife from neck to tail down the backbone.

3. Keeping the tip of the knife close against the carcass, cut the flesh away from it in scraping motions on either side of the back.

4. When you reach the legs, notice the nugget on either side known as the "oyster." This is choice meat, so be sure not to leave it behind on the bones.

5. To continue cutting below each oyster, press down on the bird with your hands to snap the legs from their sockets. The legs should now lay flat.

6. Scrape away the fat between the oyster and the tail to reveal the leg joint. Cut through.

7. Go back up to the wings and twist them to expose the joints. Cut off.

8. Remove the wishbone at the neck end.

9. Carefully continue cutting and scraping until you can pull the carcass from the breasts, leaving the breast and skin intact.

10. What you now have is the bird, flat and intact, with the legs and wings still attached.

11. If you are deboning the bird to stuff it and reconstitute the shape of the bird, as in Fruit Quail (page 138), leave the wings on (and, obviously, don't try to debone them). Take only the thighbone from each leg, and leave in the drumstick bone: This is done by making a slit in the flesh down the thighbone from its tip to the joint at the top of the drumstick. Cut through and remove. You are done.

Or, if you are deboning the bird completely to stuff and roll, as in Holiday Hen (page 135), rather than debone the legs, peel them whole from the skin, like pulling a foot out of a sock. Cut the upper wing bone out, keeping as much flesh and skin as you can, but then cut off the wing tips altogether and use with the carcass for stock. If you're not making stock right away, freeze the bones for another day.

FRUIT QUAIL

*Q*uail make perfect-sized dinner portions, especially when deboned and filled until they're almost popping their buttons with couscous, fruit, nuts, lemon, and herbs. Serve them in a nest of buttery, parsley-flecked pumpkin purée.

6 quail (about 5 ounces/150 g each)
Salt and pepper
1 to 2 tablespoons unsalted butter, melted

FOR THE SAUCE
½ leek, diced and washed
½ carrot, peeled and diced
1 shallot, diced
1 sprig parsley
1 bay leaf
4 peppercorns
2 tablespoons cold unsalted butter, cut into pieces
Salt and pepper

FOR THE STUFFING
2 tablespoons olive oil
1 small onion
1 cup/200 g cooked couscous
3 prunes, pitted and finely chopped
3 dried apricots, finely chopped
1 heaping tablespoon raisins
2 heaping tablespoons pine nuts, lightly toasted
1 garlic clove, minced
Grated zest of 1 lemon
1 to 2 tablespoons chopped fresh parsley
Salt and pepper to taste

Debone the quail from the back (see page 137), leaving in the bones in the lower part of the legs. Cover and refrigerate until using. Chop the bones and put them in a medium saucepan. Add the following sauce ingredients: leek, carrot, shallot, parsley, bay leaf, and peppercorns. Pour over cold water to cover. Bring to a boil and simmer gently 45 minutes. Strain into a small saucepan. You should have about 1 cup/250 ml stock. If you have too much, simply boil it down to that amount. Set aside.

Preheat the oven to 400°F/200°C. Take the quail from the refrigerator. Mix together all the stuffing ingredients, taste, and adjust the seasonings. Add 2 to 3 tablespoons of the stock to bind the mixture. Lay the quail out flat, season with salt and pepper, and place a few tablespoons of the stuffing in the center of each one. Fold over the breast flaps and secure with toothpicks. Tuck in the legs, securing them also. Lay the quail breast side up in a lightly oiled baking pan. Brush with the melted butter. Roast until the skin is golden and the legs pull loose easily, about 25 minutes.

Remove the quail from the pan, cover, and keep warm. Deglaze the roasting pan with the remaining stock and boil to reduce by about half. Strain into a saucepan. Whisk in the cold butter, one piece at a time, to make the sauce. Season with salt and pepper. Serve the quail with the sauce spooned over.

MON PETIT CHOU

I can't believe I'm about to say this about stuffed cabbage, but this recipe is my pride and joy. On one hand, it's old-fashioned: hearty, savory, rustic, perfect on a cold night. But, on the other, it's miraculously modern: each person gets a small and perfect leafy, meaty globe, each his own wee world, and around it is spooned light, yet richly flavored, steaming broth. It's a wondrous sight, and fun to make. Obviously you can experiment with different meats (rabbit, pork, beef, and so on), or why not work on a fish rendition? For the rich stock below, I like to use the pheasant carcass, chopped, once I've removed the meat.

1 large savoy cabbage
1 tablespoon unsalted butter
1 tablespoon olive oil
2 large onions, finely chopped
¼ pound/125 g mushrooms, finely chopped
1 to 2 tablespoons Cognac, port, or red wine
½ pound/250 g pheasant meat, finely chopped by hand
½ pound/250 g boneless veal, finely chopped by hand
2 garlic cloves, finely chopped
½ cup/20 g crumbled bread crusts
2 tablespoons chopped fresh parsley
1 tablespoon chopped fresh thyme
1 teaspoon salt
Pepper to taste
4 cups/1 l rich stock

Core the cabbage and carefully remove the leaves, keeping them whole. Bring a large pot of salted water to a boil and, working in batches, blanch the leaves until soft and pliable, about 5 minutes. Rinse immediately in cold water, drain well, and lay on tea towels to dry. Cut the thick rib from the center of each leaf and discard; this will make them look like pies with a piece missing.

Heat the butter and oil in a skillet. Sauté the onion until translucent, about 7 minutes. Add the mushrooms and cook until beginning to soften, about 5 minutes longer. Deglaze the pan with the Cognac, scraping up the good juices with a wooden spoon. Transfer to a bowl. Mix in the chopped meats, garlic, bread crumbs, parsley, thyme, salt, and pepper. Fry a piece of the mixture and taste for seasoning. Add more salt and pepper if needed. Shape the mixture into 6 or 8 balls.

Lay 2 cabbage leaves together like overlapping lily pads. Spread one portion of the stuffing down the middle across them. Starting at one end, roll over once, then fold in the sides, roll over again, and fold in the sides, and so on, until you have a rough-looking ball. Place the ball in the center of a tea towel and twist the towel around it so it looks as if you're making a puppet, the cabbage ball being the head. Keep twisting until you can twist no further and the ball is very tight inside the towel. Loosen the towel and remove the ball. Wrap a third leaf around the ball and twist again to secure. Set aside and continue making the other balls. Arrange the cabbages in a steamer basket or two.

Bring the stock to a simmer in a saucepan over which the steamer basket fits like a lid. Set on the basket(s), cover with a lid, and steam 1 hour. Remove the steamer basket, keeping it closed, and let rest while you boil down the stock to about 2 cups/500 ml. Serve the miniature cabbage globes in soup plates with their broth ladled around.

HAY HAM

[*Serves 8*]

*E*ccentricity, for better or for worse, draws me like a magnet. So a recipe like this one was bound to inspire in me a sudden obsession with finding hay (in Paris, in this century, not so easy). Weekend plans, therefore, accidentally-on-purpose got sidetracked to rural Normandy, where, apart from there being hay in abundance, were some friends who bought some organic stuff from a pet shop. Now, I know you're thinking, "What is the point?" Well, the point is: (a) you, too, are seduced by the unfathomable, and (b) hay actually does impart a unique, smoky flavor to the meat. Besides, what a scene it is when you carry to the table an enormous platter of ham nested in the hay from the cooking pot. Incidentally, if instead of smoked ham you want to use half-cured pork, such as hocks, the recipe is also good, and the soaking unnecessary.

3 pound/1.4 kg smoked ham
2 large wads clean fresh untreated hay
8 bay leaves
4 thyme sprigs (optional)

Soak the ham in cold water for 12 to 48 hours, changing the water often. Remove and pat dry.

Put half the hay in a very large pot to make a nest. Set in the ham, scatter over the bay leaves and (optional) thyme, then cover with the remaining hay. Pour in cold water to cover and bring to a boil. Lower the heat to a simmer, cover the pot, and cook until the meat falls from the bone, 4 to 5 hours.

Drain some of the hay and lay on a serving platter. Set the ham in the middle. Carve at the table.

ANCHOVY BEEF

[*Serves 6*]

My Nova Scotian grandmother used to make a dish called Salisbury Steak, which for no good reason this Languedoc recipe reminds me of, despite its inclusion of anchovies, olives, and red wine. It isn't just nostalgia that makes me crave it, though. It's the punchy flavors, the tenderness of the meat, and the casual nature of it all. This isn't fancy stuff, it's after-school food best reheated on chilly nights. Use ripe tomatoes with lots of taste, not the tennis-ball-in-disguise kind. If fresh tomatoes don't look good, use canned; they taste better.

3 tablespoons olive oil

6 medium onions, sliced

4 to 5 ounces/125 g anchovies in oil, drained, patted dry, and cut into pieces

6 garlic cloves, minced

1 large bunch parsley, chopped

A handful of fresh thyme leaves, chopped

2 pounds/1 kg tomatoes, peeled, seeded, and chopped

1 cup/160 g green olives, pitted and rinsed

Salt and pepper

1½ pounds/1.15 kg stewing beef, cut into slices about ½ inch/1 cm thick

One 750-ml bottle strong dry red wine

Preheat the oven to 325°F/160°C. Heat the oil in a large ovenproof casserole and cook the onions (on the stovetop) until very soft and melting, about 25 minutes. Meanwhile, mix together the anchovies, garlic, parsley, and thyme. Set aside. When the onions are soft, mix together with the tomatoes and olives in a bowl.

Now all the ingredients get layered in the casserole. Start with one-quarter of the onion mixture. Season with salt and pepper before layering on one-third of the meat and sprinkling over one-third of the parsley mixture. Continue making layers, ending with the onion, and not neglecting to season well between layers. Pour in the wine. Cover and braise in the oven until you can crush the meat between your fingers, about 3 hours. Serve with mashed potatoes (remembering, of course, that kept and reheated the next day, this is twice as good).

PEPPER STEAK

[*Serves 4*]

*M*y enthusiasm for steak *au poivre* never wanes. I'll take it any way you serve it, but lately I'm especially smitten with this colorful mixed-peppercorn version. Now, that's already stretching a classic, but if I don't have all the "correct" ingredients for the rest of the recipe, I'm not above cheating even more. For example, last time I had no Cognac and so used red wine. That didn't seem to do any harm. I've been without beef stock, too, and used chicken stock from a cube instead. It was excellent, too. For the clarified butter below: melt butter, skim off the foam that rises to the top, and pour off the clear butter, leaving the milky residue behind.

3 heaping tablespoons mixed peppercorns (black, green, and white)
1 heaping tablespoon pink peppercorns
4 pieces thick boneless rib-eye or sirloin steak (about ¼ pound/125 g each)
1 garlic clove, split
Salt
3 to 4 tablespoons clarified butter
½ cup/125 ml beef stock
¼ cup/60 ml Cognac
½ cup/125 ml heavy cream

If you have time, soak the mixed peppercorns (not the pink ones) in ½ cup/125 ml red wine or tea for a few hours to soften. If you don't have time, this will be ultra-peppery, but some people (me, for example) like it like that too. Drain well and combine with the pink peppercorns. Crush slightly under a heavy saucepan.

Rub the steaks with the garlic and season with salt. Coat each steak with the peppercorns, pressing them against the meat with your hands so that they cling. Heat the butter until sizzling in a skillet large enough to hold all the steaks comfortably. Fry to the doneness of your liking, 2 to 3 minutes per side for me. Remove to serving plates.

Deglaze the pan with the beef stock, scraping up the good bits from the bottom. Boil to reduce by half. Add the Cognac. Set a match to the pan (carefully) to bring the alcohol dazzlingly alight. When the flames die down, add the cream and swirl it around. Boil to reduce to sauce consistency. Taste, and season the sauce (no salt if you've used stock-cube stock). Pour over the steaks, and serve.

ROAST BEEF

[*Serves 6 to 8*]

Two of my favorite home cooks, friends Léon and Gigi, reminded me of the joys of a good roast beef. One Saturday night at their place we had it served in thick rare slabs with heaps of Léon's shallot sauce. Then on Sunday, I went back again for leftovers, and this time Gigi served it cold with swirls of her thick, heady walnut mayonnaise and a green salad. So, I don't know what to tell you. Roast lots, I guess, so you're guaranteed both options.

One 3-pound/1.4-kg prime rib roast
Salt and pepper
Shallot sauce (recipe follows)

Bring the meat to room temperature on the counter, about 30 minutes.

Preheat the oven to 450°F/230°C. Rub the roast all over with salt and pepper. Set in a roasting pan and roast 30 minutes.

Check for doneness. The meat should be rare to medium at this point, slightly spongy to the touch. If you like meat more well done, return it to the oven and check every 10 minutes, until it's just shy of being cooked to your liking. Remove the roast from the oven and let rest 10 minutes before carving. Serve with the sauce.

SHALLOT SAUCE

[*Makes about 1 cup/250 ml*]

This is thick and buttery rich, but you're going to eat way more of it than you plan. With plain roasted meat, it is supremely good. Any left over can be heated up and tossed with pasta or added to a savory tart.

½ pound/250 g shallots, very thinly sliced
2 cups/500 ml white wine, more if necessary
5 tablespoons unsalted butter, softened
2 garlic cloves, chopped
1 to 2 teaspoons *herbes de Provence*
Salt and pepper

Put the shallots in a medium saucepan and pour over enough wine to cover completely; if you don't have enough, top up with water. Bring to a boil and cook until the wine has disappeared and the shallots are soft, about 45 minutes. Remove the pan from the heat and beat in the butter piece by piece; you want the butter to get hot and meld with the shallots, but not melt into them. Stir in the garlic and herbs. Season with salt and pepper. Serve warm with sliced roast beef.

LAMB TAGINE

*T*his recipe belongs to my good friend Randall Price, and did I ever find out the hard way. He taught me to make his tagine once when I needed an impressive dish for a special dinner. Later, I wrote the recipe into my kitchen notebook and then forgot about it, despite the fact that his magnificent tagine had earned my cooking a fine reputation. Three years later, I showed up with the main course for a New Year's Eve dinner at Randall's and proudly introduced to him my contribution: "*my* lamb tagine." "Yours!" he yelled. "You recipe thief, that's mine!" I still haven't lived it down. But, honestly, credit for his recipe I'd never want to steal. Can't say I regret making off with the recipe itself though.

2 pounds/1 kg lamb shoulder, cut into 1-inch (2.5-cm) cubes
Salt and pepper

FOR THE MARINADE
4 medium-to-large onions, chopped
4 garlic cloves, minced
3 tablespoons cumin
1 tablespoon paprika
1 tablespoon chopped fresh ginger
1 teaspoon ground ginger
1 teaspoon cinnamon
1 teaspoon ground coriander
1 teaspoon turmeric
2 pinches saffron
Pinch of cayenne pepper
1 cinnamon stick
1 tablespoon honey
1 dried orange peel (leave the peel from an orange out to dry overnight)
½ cup/125 ml olive oil

4 red peppers
One 32-oz/850-g can tomatoes
Peels of 4 preserved lemons, finely chopped
¾ cup/125 g black olives, pitted
¾ cup/135 g blanched whole almonds, toasted
2 large handfuls chopped fresh cilantro

Two to three days before you plan to serve the dish, season the meat generously with salt and pepper and place in a large glass bowl. Add all the marinade ingredients and toss to coat well. Cover with plastic wrap and refrigerate for 24 to 48 hours.

To cook the tagine, bring the meat to room temperature. Preheat the oven to broil, and broil the red peppers on a baking sheet, turning so that they blacken on all sides, about 15 minutes total. Remove them to a plastic bag and close the bag to steam for 5 minutes.

Lower the oven temperature to 325°F/150°C. Now the pepper skins will peel off with ease. Peel, seed, and slice the peppers into julienne strips, then add to the meat. Transfer the meat mixture to a lidded casserole. Add the tomatoes, half the preserved lemon, and the olives. Bring to a boil on the stovetop. Cover tightly, transfer to the oven, and bake until the lamb is crushingly tender, about 2 hours.

Uncover, and return to a burner. Boil to reduce the cooking juices until you obtain a thick stew, about 15 minutes. Cool completely, cover, and refrigerate overnight.

To serve the tagine, reheat it. When bubbling, pour into a warm serving dish. Scatter over the almonds, cilantro, and the remaining lemon. Bring to the table with heaps of buttery couscous and a big bowl of Minted Lettuce Peas (page 176) to serve on the side.

POT ON THE FIRE

*I*rish stew's French cousin is how I think of *pot-au-feu*. Although not entirely alike, both fill the kitchen with the same homey aromas and comfort hungry bellies in the dead of winter. I had no trouble getting six rather fashionable women around my table (and on a Saturday night!) just to eat my unapologetically unfashionable *pot-au-feu*. We followed it with salad and cheese, then Hot Chocolate (page 208), and everybody left at one in the morning, as full of good gossip as anything else. Traditional garnishes for Pot on the Fire are individual bowls of horseradish, gherkins, capers, mustard, red currant jelly, and pickled beets.

3 pounds/1.4 kg lean beef, such as shin, tied in a log

2 pounds/1 kg fatter cut of beef, such as belly or flank, tied in a log

8 medium-to-small onions, peeled

4 celery stalks, cut into 4-inch pieces (in North America only; French celery is too strong)

3 bay leaves

3 parsley sprigs

3 thyme sprigs

8 peppercorns, tied in a piece of muslin

1 tablespoon coarse salt

8 whites of leek, tied in a bundle

8 large carrots, halved

8 parsnips, halved, or ½ celeriac bulb, peeled and cut into chunks

8 medium potatoes, peeled and quartered

Chopped fresh parsley

Put the meat in a large stewing pot and pour over cold water to cover. Bring to a simmer very slowly; when a scum starts rising, skim it off. Keep simmering and skimming until no more scum appears, about 15 minutes. Add the onions, celery, herbs, pepper pouch, and salt. Cover, tilting the lid a bit to let steam escape. Bring barely back to a simmer and stew gently for 2 hours.

Add the leeks, carrots, and parsnips. Continue simmering 2 hours longer.

When everything is tender and the broth rich, remove the meat and vegetables to a dish, cool, and cover. Strain the broth through a cloth into a clean pot. Cool, and cover also. Refrigerate both dishes overnight.

The next day, skim off any fat that has risen and set on the top of the broth. Bring the broth to a boil, taste, and season with salt and pepper. Return the solids to the pot and add the potatoes. Simmer until the potatoes are tender and the meat and other vegetables heated through. Serve hot, sprinkled with chopped fresh parsley.

SIDE DISHES

A lot of fuss is made over pairing wine with food, and not enough over pairing food with food itself. I didn't use to give it much conscious thought either. When I made a meat dish, I'd just slap alongside a vegetable, any vegetable, and tick off the side-dish box in my brain. I've since learned that a well-thought-out side dish can profoundly enhance the food it accompanies.

While there's no formula in choosing them, there is a mantra: balance. And that's what you want humming in your mind when you plot a single plate, as when you design an entire menu. Consider not only taste but also texture, color, weight, and so on. You want to avoid doing what I once did, which was to serve a five-course dinner, every dish of which contained some form of cheese. Be careful with contrasts too. There's a fine line between variety and chaos.

Finally, don't assume side dishes are secondary. There are times when you'll luck into perfect baby green beans in the market. Let them dictate the main course rather than the other way around. The cooking method is directed by quality too. When summer tomatoes hit the stands, plump, ripe, and juicy, leave them raw and drizzle over a few threads of oil, rather than stewing them. If you see that the carrots are looking a little limp, purée them, or make them into a flan. Nothing can be perfect all the time, but you can make the most of produce by putting thought into how you cook it and how its main accompaniment will harmonize with it.

ALSATIAN POTATO SALAD

[*Serves 4*]

My version of this classic, based on a recipe from Chef Anton Edelmann's book *Fast Feasts,* has been with me for years. Back in my university days, it was practically my trademark dish: I used to triple the recipe and cart it out to the leafy, walled park behind my residence for barbecues and birthdays. Maybe nostalgia, then, is the reason I always think of this as outdoor food. It's meant to be served warm, actually, and I do like it best that way, but the world doesn't end if you eat it at room temperature.

1¼ pounds/625 g new waxy potatoes, unpeeled
1 cup/¼ pound/125 g shelled peas
¼ pound/125 g bacon, cut into pieces
1 medium red onion, chopped
1 garlic clove, minced
¼ cup/60 ml white wine vinegar
¼ cup/60 ml chicken stock
½ cup/125 ml grapeseed or vegetable oil
Salt and pepper

Boil the potatoes in a large pot of salted water until tender. Drain, peel, and slice (¼-inch/5-mm slices) into a large bowl. Meanwhile, boil the peas in a saucepan of boiling salted water until tender. Rinse immediately under cold water, drain, and set aside.

Fry the bacon in a frying pan. When crisp, add the onion and garlic and stir to warm through. Pour over the vinegar to deglaze, scraping up the good bits from the bottom of the pan. Stir in the stock and oil. Add the peas to warm through. Then combine all with the potatoes in the bowl. Season with salt and pepper, and serve.

POTATO GRATIN

A friend whose family farms garlic on the Isle of Wight once brought me a gift of smoked garlic and I was, in one whiff of those fumes, sent into seventh heaven. Potato gratin is a perfect way to show it off. If you can't buy smoked garlic, the ordinary kind is excellent in this recipe too; it's what I use most often. But I'd like to find out more about the smoked stuff, and wonder if garlic heads couldn't simply be slow-smoked over wood chips at home. At any rate, depending on what you use in this recipe, adjust the garlic quantity to suit your taste. Don't hesitate to add grated cheese to the center if you're in the mood for a richer dish.

2 pounds/1 kg waxy potatoes, peeled and thinly sliced
Salt and pepper
Pinch of nutmeg (optional)
About ½ head garlic, cloves peeled and grated
1 cup/250 ml milk
1 cup/250 ml heavy cream
1 to 2 tablespoons unsalted butter

Preheat the oven to 375°F/190°C. Spill half the potato slices into a gratin dish. Season well with salt, pepper, and nutmeg, if desired. Smear over the grated garlic. Spread over the remaining potato slices. Pour over the milk and cream. Season well again with salt and pepper. Dot with the butter. Bake until all the liquid has been absorbed and the top is bubbly brown, 1 to 1½ hours. Serve.

OLIVE POTATOES

[*Serves 4*]

I have an excellent book on vegetables called *Etonnants Légumes* (*Amazing Vegetables*) by Thierry Thorens, which is packed with inventive ideas for serving things that sound familiar, but then suddenly aren't. This potato dish is one of many that grabbed my attention. I suppose it's not all that far out, but when someone says "potato" the tongue just doesn't expect those crunchy pine nuts, that pungent squoosh of garlic, and the salty bite of olives.

½ cup/125 ml olive oil
2 pounds/1 kg waxy potatoes, cut into ½-inch/1-cm rounds
4 medium onions, sliced
8 garlic cloves, unpeeled
Salt and pepper
2 to 4 thyme sprigs
½ cup/50 g black olives, pitted
½ cup/50 g green olives, pitted
½ cup/60 g pine nuts
A generous handful of shredded fresh basil

Heat the olive oil in a large sauté pan until quite hot. Add the potatoes, onions, and garlic, stirring to coat. Season with salt and pepper, and add the thyme sprigs. Cook uncovered, stirring occasionally, until the onions are soft and the potatoes tender and golden, about 30 minutes.

Toss in the olives and pine nuts, stirring to warm them. Check the seasonings. Toss in the basil, then tilt all into a serving bowl.

FRIES

*A*mong the amusing signs one spots on French roadways is the supremely optimistic *"Toutes Directions"* ("All Directions") and inevitably, a few meters later, that relieving alternative, *"Autres Directions"* ("Other Directions"). I wish all life were that simple. *"FRITES"* is another of my favorite signs. There it is scrawled in big black letters on a board and poked into the ground in the unlikeliest of spots: by a field of sunflowers, at the entrance to a narrow dirt turnoff, half hidden in a ditch outside town. "Where are those frites?!" I always wonder, because never once have I actually seen a truck parked on the spot to sell them, which presumably is how the system works. So, my own *frites* I must make.

6 large starchy potatoes
About 8 cups/2 l peanut oil
Salt

Peel and trim the ends from the potatoes. Cut into ¼-inch/6-mm sticks. Keep them in a bowl covered with cold water until using.

Drain the potatoes well and pat dry with a tea towel before frying. There are two frying stages: First heat the oil in a deep-fryer or high-sided saucepan to 325°F/160°C. The oil will be bubbling on the surface, but not in a mad froth. Blanch the potatoes in batches until soft and limp, about 5 minutes. Remove with a perforated spoon to paper towels to drain. You can prepare the potatoes to this stage up to 2 hours before the final cooking.

To finish, heat the oil to 375°F/190°C. Now it will be bubbling quite aggressively. Fry the potatoes a second time, in batches, until very crisp and well browned, 2 to 3 minutes. Remove to paper towels to drain. Season with salt just before serving.

PURÉED VEGETABLES

*E*verybody likes baby food, as a friend of mine puts it. I'm not sure how flattering it is to have it spelled out in quite those terms, but I admit that the smoothness, the bright colors, and the purity of flavors are qualities of purées that I've never grown out of loving. Besides, I like playing with the leftovers: transforming them into vegetable flans (page 72), soufflés (page 76), or steaming cream soups.

The most obvious purée is **potato**. That may sound boring until you start getting friendly with the idea of pressing the final results at least once through a fine-meshed sieve or food mill for ultrasmoothness. Starchy potatoes, rather than waxy, are a must. They should be boiled, with their skins left on in salted water, drained, and peeled immediately afterward (rubber gloves come in handy around hot potatoes, by the way). Then you sieve the warm potatoes through a ricer or a mesh sieve. Whip in melted butter, boiling milk, salt, and pepper until they're smooth and flavorful, although you needn't stop there. You might like to swirl through a bit of pesto, tapenade, grainy Dijon mustard, or horseradish. Or add a good handful of finely chopped fresh herbs. And don't forget that potatoes can be combined with another vegetable in purée, celeriac being a classic partner.

White bean is another purée great, and I'm a fan because not only is this an ideal accompaniment to lamb chops, but it can also be eaten on its own, smeared warm on toast, drizzled with olive oil, and sprinkled with lots of ground pepper. First, cover 2 cups/500 g white beans in cold water, soak overnight, and drain. Then sauté 2 chopped shallots with 2 chopped garlic cloves in a tablespoon of olive oil until soft. Stir in the beans and add a bay leaf and a sprig or two of thyme. Pour over chicken stock or water to cover, bring to a boil, slap on a lid, and simmer gently until the beans are very tender, 45 minutes at least. Drain the beans, reserving the liquid. Pluck out the bay and thyme. Purée with however much of the cooking liquid is needed to achieve a smooth, thick consistency.

Whip in a few spoonfuls of melted butter or olive oil. Season well with salt and pepper, and serve nice and warm. (This makes 2 cups/500 ml.)

Other vegetables (and all you do is boil or steam them, then mash while still hot) are, for instance: squash, peas, turnip, pumpkin, parsnip, celeriac, Jerusalem artichoke, green beans, carrots, chestnuts, cauliflower, lentils, and beets. Their purées are prepared the same way as potato, but you could replace the milk in some cases with cream, or with stock. You might want a dash of vinegar, wine, or a flavored oil to add interest. Various spices can give purées new life; cumin is classic with carrot and cauliflower, for instance. And herbs can be puréed with the vegetable or a chopped handful stirred into the purée afterward. For a more rustic take, crush rather than mush the vegetables, and mix in olive oil rather than butter and cream.

TABBOULEH

Nobody's pretending that this is authentic tabbouleh of the Middle Eastern sort, but it is the way many French cooks (and I) make and like to eat it. A good trick here is that the couscous (more common in French tabbouleh recipes than bulgur) is not cooked, but simply plumped in lemon juice and olive oil, which means the grains never go clumpy, even after a day or two in the fridge. And I do like a day or two's worth in there for pillaging at lunch. Tabbouleh is also a good accompaniment for grilled chicken or meat.

2 cups/350 g quick-cooking couscous
¾ cup/175 ml lemon juice, or more to taste
¾ cup/175 ml olive oil
At least ½ cup/¾ ounce finely chopped fresh parsley, more if desired
At least ½ cup/¾ ounce finely chopped fresh mint, more if desired
2 medium tomatoes, seeded and chopped
1 red pepper, seeded and chopped
1 medium onion, minced
Salt and pepper

Stir together the couscous, lemon juice, and olive oil. Set aside to plump and soften, 1 to 2 hours at room temperature, stirring occasionally. It's ready when the grains are pleasantly al dente.

Stir in the herbs, tomatoes, red pepper, and onion. Season with salt and pepper. Add lemon juice to taste. Cover and refrigerate overnight. Serve the next day.

RAINBOW RICE

*I*ngredients lists can be deceiving. Here, for example, they're all foods we've been eating ever since we cut our teeth, but somehow when combined into a textured confetti with a tangy kick of lemon, they lose their familiarity and take on a different charm. Add chopped parsley, cilantro, or mint to the salad if you like.

1 cup/250 g rice
¼ cup/30 g peas
¼ cup diced red pepper
¼ cup diced carrot
¼ cup diced zucchini
1 celery stalk, thinly sliced
1 medium tomato
¼ cup/60 ml olive oil
1 to 2 teaspoons Dijon mustard
1 tablespoon white wine vinegar
Salt and pepper
Grated zest of 2 large lemons

Bring a pot of salted water to a boil. Cook the rice until al dente. Drain. Immediately rinse in cold water to stop the cooking. Drain well. Set aside.

Prepare a smaller saucepan of boiling salted water for the vegetables. Have a perforated spoon or small sieve at the ready to scoop them out, and set a colander in the sink. First blanch the peas. Scoop them out and rinse immediately under very cold water to stop the cooking. Put them in a medium bowl. Bring the water back to a boil and blanch, each in turn, the red pepper, carrot, and zucchini, taking care to bring the water back to a boil between each; leave the celery raw. Add them all to the bowl with the peas.

Bring the water to a boil one last time. Carve an X into the bottom of the tomato. Plunge into the water for 12 seconds, then remove and plunge into ice-cold water. Peel, seed, and dice. Combine with the other vegetables.

Make the vinaigrette by whisking together the mustard and vinegar, then adding the oil in a thin drizzle. Season with salt and pepper. Stir in the lemon zest. Mix together with the rice and vegetables in a serving bowl. Let sit for about an hour at room temperature before serving.

SUMMER LENTILS

[*Serves 6*]

*T*here are two reasons why this is my hot-weather lentil dish: first, it's light and lively with grilled fish off the barbecue, and second, my idea of winter lentils is other. I'll just tell you quickly so you've got a replacement for this once the leaves change color and start flying off in the wind. Fry a chopped big red onion in olive oil with some chopped garlic. Add the same quantity of lentils as below, a bay leaf, and a thyme sprig. Cover with water and simmer until tender, draining off any unabsorbed water at the end. Season well with salt and pepper, then dress with balsamic vinegar, olive oil, and walnut oil. Stir in toasted walnuts and generous pinches of fresh goat's cheese, then pile onto winter greens and dig in.

1 cup/250 g French green lentils (lentilles du Puy)
2 to 3 medium tomatoes
1 large carrot, peeled and diced
1 red pepper, seeded and diced
2 tablespoons balsamic vinegar
1 teaspoon Dijon mustard
7 tablespoons olive oil
2 shallots, minced
Salt and pepper
2 large handfuls chopped fresh chives

Rinse the lentils well in cold water and put them in a saucepan with 1½ cups/375 ml water. Bring to a boil, cover, and simmer until the lentils are al dente, 30 to 40 minutes. Drain and reserve.

While the lentils cook, bring a pot of salted water to a boil. Cut an X in the skin at the bottom of the tomatoes and plunge them into the water for 12 seconds. Immediately scoop them from the water (leaving the water on the heat) and rinse under cold water to stop the cooking. Peel, quarter, and seed the tomatoes. Dice the flesh.

Now throw the carrot dice into the boiling water and cook until al dente, just a few minutes. Scoop the carrots out and rinse under ice-cold water. Set aside. Follow the same procedure with the red pepper. Discard the water.

For the vinaigrette, whisk together the vinegar and mustard, then whisk in the oil in a thin drizzle. Stir in the shallots. Season with salt and pepper. Combine the lentils, vegetables, vinaigrette, and chives in a serving bowl. Check the seasonings. Let sit for an hour at room temperature before serving.

ROASTED VEGETABLES

[*Serves 6*]

Virtually all vegetables are superb roasted, and I change my combinations every time. In this mix, the cherry tomatoes may at first seem out of place, but once roasted, they become intense in flavor, almost candied, melding with the garlic and rosemary-infused oil, and giving a surprising lift to the mix of mostly roots. Remember that exact timing for roasting vegetables depends on what size you cut the vegetables. Remember, too, that a spice mix is nice sometimes instead of herbs; you might consider choosing from five-spice powder, fennel seeds, paprika, allspice, tandoori spice mix, cumin, or some combination thereof.

6 medium potatoes, cut into chunks
6 small carrots, peeled and halved lengthwise
2 leeks, trimmed, washed, and cut into chunks
2 generous handfuls cherry tomatoes
2 heads garlic, broken into cloves and peeled
Coarse sea salt and freshly cracked black pepper
¼ cup/60 ml olive oil
3 rosemary branches
3 bay leaves
2 tablespoons unsalted butter

Preheat the oven to 400°F/200°C. Put all the vegetables, with the garlic, in a roasting pan. Season with salt and pepper, and pour over the oil. Toss with your hands to coat well. Tuck the herbs in and around the vegetables. Dot the butter on top. Roast until the vegetables are soft inside and caramelized and crisping outside, 1 to 1½ hours. Serve hot.

TOMATO EGGPLANT GRATIN

[*Serves 6*]

Most recipes I've seen for this sort of gratin call for the eggplant to be breaded and fried in lots of oil. I have nothing against the taste, but I find it makes a soggy mess (or, rather, *I* make the soggy mess). So, to spare my kitchen and my ego that disaster, I grill the eggplant in the oven instead. Sometimes, I stop right there: grilled eggplant with a bit of olive oil makes an excellent side dish in its own right. But the times I carry on with the full-meal deal, below, I'm pretty satisfied with myself. The dish is fabulous hot the night of making, or at room temperature for lunch the next day too.

About ½ cup/125 ml olive oil
2 large onions, chopped
3 garlic cloves, chopped
4 pounds/1.8 kg tomatoes, roughly chopped
1 bay leaf
Salt and pepper
A handful of fresh herb leaves such as basil, parsley, or rosemary, or all three, chopped
2 pounds/1 kg eggplant, cut into ½-inch/1-cm slices
About 1 cup/80 g homemade bread crumbs, toasted
Pinch of chili powder, or more to taste
About 3 tablespoons freshly grated Parmigiano-Reggiano

Preheat the oven to 450°F/230°C. Heat 2 tablespoons of the olive oil in a sauté pan and cook the onions until soft, about 10 minutes. Add the garlic, tomatoes, and bay leaf. Cook, uncovered, into a thick sauce, about 45 minutes. Remove the bay leaf, season with salt and pepper, and stir in the fresh herbs.

Meanwhile, brush the eggplant slices on both sides with olive oil, and lay in a single layer on a baking sheet (you'll have to do two or three batches). Grill until softened and golden on top, about 15 minutes; turn and grill the other side about 10 minutes. Remove and set aside. Turn the oven down to 375°F/190°C. Mix together the bread crumbs and chili powder.

In a large gratin dish, starting with just the thinnest smear of tomato sauce over the bottom, make layers of your preparations: first overlapping eggplant, then tomato sauce, then bread crumbs; then start from the beginning again. When the dish is full, scatter over the cheese. Bake until the gratin is heated through and the top golden, about 30 minutes. Serve.

RATATOUILLE

Ratatouille is still exotic to me, a glossy pageant of eggplant purple, tomato red, zucchini green, parsley, rosemary, and basil, all glistening together under a slippery veil of olive oil. As if that weren't enough, it's also a practical dish: you can eat it hot or at room temperature, as a starter or a side dish, on its own or spooned into a tart shell and baked, or wrapped in a blanket of Buckwheat Galettes (page 111). The other bonus is that ratatouille can restore to glory vegetables that may be a little past their prime. In fact, some people insist that it's better when made with slightly overripe vegetables. A ratatouille variation is to brush the vegetables with olive oil and grill them in sequence; at the end, season with salt and pepper, and stir in herbs. This makes a drier version that's also very nice.

2½ pounds/1.2 kg tomatoes
About ½ cup/125 ml olive oil, more if necessary
2 medium onions, sliced
4 garlic cloves, chopped; more if you want
1 bay leaf
1 rosemary branch
2 thyme sprigs
¼ cup/60 ml tomato paste
5 zucchini (about 2 pounds/1 kg), sliced
3 red peppers, seeded and chopped
3 eggplants (about 1½ pounds/750 g), sliced
Salt and pepper
A handful of chopped fresh parsley
A handful of chopped fresh basil

Preheat the oven to 450°F/230°C. Bring a large pot of water to a boil. Carve an X in the bottom of the tomatoes. When the water boils, plunge in the tomatoes a few at a time and count 12 seconds. Pull them out and rinse immediately under cold water. Now you can peel them easily, flick out the seeds, and roughly chop.

Heat a tablespoon of the olive oil in a sauté pan and cook the onions until soft and translucent, about 10 minutes. Add the 4 garlic cloves and cook 1 minute. Add the tomatoes, along with the bay leaf, rosemary branch, and thyme sprigs. Stir in the tomato concentrate. Cook gently until the tomatoes become a thick, chunky sauce, about 30 minutes. Remove to a bowl, plucking out the herbs.

Wipe the sauté pan clean, heat another tablespoon of oil, and sauté the zucchini, working again in batches, until soft. Add to the tomatoes.

While the tomatoes and then the zucchini are cooking, put the red peppers in the oven and roast, turning occasionally, until the skins blacken on all sides, about 20 minutes. Remove to a plastic bag, close, and let steam a few minutes. Peel, seed, and slice into strips. Next, brush both sides of the eggplant slices with olive oil, lay the slices on a baking sheet, and bake until soft and beginning to brown, about 15 minutes. Turn and continue cooking 10 minutes. (If your oven is large enough, roast the peppers and eggplant simultaneously.)

Add the eggplant and peppers to the tomatoes. Season the mixture with salt and pepper. Add the parsley and basil. Add extra chopped garlic if you like, and a drizzle of olive oil. Serve warm or at room temperature.

MIXED JULIENNE

[*Serves 4 to 6*]

*O*ften enough it's the leftovers I'm grateful for, at the end of a day when I come in so ravenous I could eat the fridge itself. What bliss to fling open its door and find a colorful, frenzied heap in there of healthy vegetables, hot in three minutes, and superb with a magnanimous grating of Parmigiano-Reggiano. That's the leftovers, but mixed julienne the first time round is pretty fast too, although there's a bit of a knife-skill–improvement session before cooking: cutting the vegetables into matchstick-sized julienne. Serve as a bed for fish. And do vary the vegetables according to your own whims and the seasons.

2 leeks, trimmed and washed
2 large carrots, peeled
2 small zucchini
2 tablespoons olive oil
2 tablespoons unsalted butter
Salt and pepper
Lemon juice to taste

Cut the vegetables into fine julienne strips. Heat the oil and butter in a sauté pan. Add the vegetables and cook gently, tossing occasionally, until soft, about 5 minutes. Season with salt, pepper, and lemon juice. Serve.

SPRING RAGOUT

[*Serves 4*]

*W*hen the first fava beans and asparagus hit the shops in spring, this fresh ragout is the first thing I make. There are a few eye-appealing ways to go about the recipe. The method calls for the tender green vegetables to be tossed with bacon and a light fresh goat's cheese cream sauce, great with grilled lamb or pork chops. If I'm already serving a creamy dish, then I leave out the cream and bacon, and simply toss the vegetables in the warm butter with the chervil. And if I'm serving the dish as a starter where I want to show off the green of the vegetables without giving up the sauce, I spoon the goat's cheese cream into soup plates and arrange the chervil and bacon-flecked vegetables in a bountiful heap on top.

2 pounds/1 kg fava beans, shelled
⅓ pound/165 g asparagus tips, or fine green beans, trimmed and halved
1 cup/150 g peas
⅓ cup/80 ml heavy cream
2 ounces/60 g fresh goat's cheese
Salt and pepper
2 tablespoons unsalted butter
3 strips bacon, more if desired, fried and crumbled
A handful of chopped fresh chervil

Bring a large pot of salted water to a boil. Blanch the fava beans 1 to 2 minutes. Scoop them out and immediately plunge into ice-cold water. Drain, peel, and set aside. Blanch and cool the asparagus (or green beans), and the peas in the same way. All should have taken on various shades of bright green and be cooked al dente.

Heat the cream and goat's cheese in a small saucepan until the cheese has melted and the sauce is thick and bubbling. Season with salt and pepper. Melt the butter in a sauté pan until foaming. Add the vegetables, and toss to coat and heat through. Stir in the cream. Taste, and adjust the seasonings. Scatter over the bacon and chervil. Serve warm.

BUTTERY TWO TOMATOES

[*Serves 4*]

Use cherry tomatoes here if you'd rather, or larger tomatoes halved and cooked cut side down. Any way, their sweet, buttery juices, with the denser chewiness of their sun-dried cousins, make a wonderful accompaniment for grilled chicken or fish. I like the leftovers too, hot on rice, for supper in a bowl just for me.

¼ cup/60 g unsalted butter
6 medium tomatoes, thickly sliced
6 ounces/165 g soft sun-dried tomatoes, drained if oil-packed
Salt and pepper

Melt the butter in a large sauté pan over medium heat. Lay in the tomatoes and scatter the sun-dried tomatoes over the top. Cover and cook until the fresh tomatoes are soft but still holding their form, about 10 minutes. Uncover, and continue cooking to reduce the juices, if necessary. Season with salt and pepper. Serve warm.

ENDIVES WITH HONEY AND GOLDEN RAISINS

[*Serves 4*]

*H*owever simple sounding, this is an ambrosial combination: caramelized, sticky raisins, slippery, crunchy endive, and a hint of honey. With fish, I recommend adding a squirt of lemon at the very end. And if there are no honey and raisins in the house, endive with just butter alone, caramelizing in a pan, does it for me. In that case, though, I halve or quarter the endives instead of slicing and I cover them to cook.

8 to 10 endives
2 tablespoons unsalted butter
¾ cup/100 g golden raisins
1 tablespoon honey
Salt and pepper

Trim, chop, wash, and drain the endives. Melt the butter in a sauté pan over high heat, add the raisins, and heat for about half a minute, shaking the pan as they begin to caramelize. Add the endives and sauté, stirring occasionally, until soft and turning golden at the edges. Add the honey, season with salt and pepper, and serve.

GREEN BEANS WITH SHALLOTS
AND TOASTED ALMONDS

[*Serves 4 to 6*]

The ways with sautéed green beans are endless. Sometimes I throw in cherry tomatoes right up front with the beans, so that their skins crack and crinkle and their insides turn gooey and sweet; to that I probably add chopped garlic too. Other times ginger and a splash of soy sauce or balsamic vinegar is the way to go. However, this simple union of almond slivers and shallot is the garnish I like most often. The subtle toasted, nutty crunch against slender, supple beans goes irresistibly well with many main dishes.

1 lb/500 g green beans
¼ cup/20 g slivered almonds
1 tablespoon unsalted butter
1 tablespoon olive oil
1 to 2 shallots, chopped
Salt and pepper

Set a large pot of salted water on to boil. While you wait, trim the green beans, and gently toast the almonds in a large dry sauté pan. When the water is plumping, throw in the beans, which will stop the boiling. As soon as the water comes back to a boil, drain the beans and rinse under ice-cold water. Drain well, and pat dry with a towel.

Heat the butter and oil in the sauté pan, add the beans, and cook, turning occasionally, until limp, about 10 minutes. Three to five minutes before the beans reach the stage of doneness you like (Americans tend to like them on the crunchy side, the French prefer them cooked a little more), add the chopped shallots. Season with salt and pepper, toss in the toasted almonds, and take the beans to the table.

CARROT JUICE CARROTS

[*Serves 6*]

*L*eftover juice from Carrot Juice Chicken (page 90) got swooshed one night into a sauté pan of carrots, producing one of the most stunning side dishes I've ever seen, not to mention one of the most powerfully flavored. Tuna in Fragrant Water (page 126) just doesn't ever get made without these carrots in their sunshiny juices. Toss with a bit of chopped fresh herb, such as basil, parsley, or dill.

2 pounds/1 kg carrots, peeled and thickly sliced
2 tablespoons unsalted butter
1½ cups/375 ml carrot juice
Salt and pepper

Put the carrots in a sauté pan. Add the butter and juice. Pour over enough cold water to just cover. Season with salt and pepper. Bring to a simmer, and cook until the juices have reduced to syrup and the carrots are tender, about 25 minutes. Serve.

MINTED LETTUCE PEAS

[*Serves 4 to 6*]

When I serve Lamb Tagine (page 149), these peas are a sure accompaniment. And quite a sight they are, too: mossy round peas with grassy threads of lettuce twisting through like stretches of tulle, then bright sequins of fresh mint. It's a nice change from the norm, but if you're in a rush, try a simpler, sprightlier dish: toss plain boiled peas in butter, salt, pepper, and chopped fresh mint. If you've never done this before, you'll be amazed at how much character the herb imparts. Both versions are good with fish or poached chicken too.

3 tablespoons unsalted butter
1 large onion, chopped
Salt and pepper
3 cups/450 g peas
1 head Boston lettuce, separated into leaves
A generous handful of chopped fresh mint

Melt the butter in a sauté pan and gently fry the onion until soft and translucent, about 15 minutes. Season with salt and pepper. Pour over about ¼ cup/60 ml water and bring to a boil. Add the peas, tossing to coat, cover, and cook until tender, 12 to 15 minutes.

Meanwhile, trim away any hard white bits of rib from the lettuce leaves. Working in batches, pile leaves on top of one another, roll into a log, and shred with a knife. You'll finish with an unnervingly large pile of shredded lettuce strands, but they'll cook down.

Remove the lid from the peas and add the lettuce. Continue cooking, uncovered, until the peas are completely soft, the lettuce strands wilted, and the water evaporated, about 5 minutes. Correct the seasonings. Stir in as much mint as suits your taste. Serve.

LEMON SPINACH

[*Serves 4*]

*L*emon zest gives deep forest green leaves of spinach a fresh lift, excellent with fish and pork in particular. Experiment with mixed zests (grapefruit, lime, orange, lemon), and try toasted sesame seeds tossed in sometime too.

1 pound/500 g spinach
1 tablespoon unsalted butter
1 tablespoon olive oil
Grated zest of 1 lemon
Salt and pepper

Remove and discard the stems from the spinach. Wash and drain the leaves, leaving the little water that clings to them. Heat the butter and oil together in a sauté pan. Add the spinach in a big heap, cover, and cook 3 minutes.

Uncover and continue cooking, turning occasionally, until the spinach has wilted and the water evaporated. Remove the pan from the heat. Stir in the lemon zest, and season well with salt and pepper.

GINGER ONION CHARD

[*Serves 4*]

*E*ver since first tasting chard cooked this way, I've been a regular patron. The method uses both the long flat ivory stems and the floppy wintergreen leaves, cooked in peanut oil, which is a surprisingly nice change from olive oil and butter. I like this chard with red and white meats both.

2 pounds/1 kg Swiss chard
About 3 tablespoons peanut or safflower oil
1 large onion, chopped
4 garlic cloves, minced
1-inch/2.5-cm piece fresh ginger, peeled and grated
Salt and pepper
A squeeze of lemon, or to taste

Separate the chard leaves from the stems. Wash the stems, halve them lengthwise, and slice very thin. Stack the leaves in batches, roll up, and shred with a knife. Rinse the leaves in a sink of ice-cold water and shake off most of the water.

Heat the oil in a wok or large sauté pan. Gently cook the onion with the garlic and ginger until soft and lightly golden, about 15 minutes. Add the chard stems, stirring to combine, and season with salt and pepper. Cook until approaching tender, about 15 minutes. Add the leaves, stirring again to combine, and continue cooking until the leaves have wilted and the stems are completely cooked, about 10 minutes longer. Check the seasonings, adding a squirt of lemon to taste, and serve.

BACONY BRUSSELS SPROUTS LEAVES

[*Serves 4*]

*M*ore than one French cook has insisted to me that Brussels spouts must never be blanched in water, but simply sautéed in butter and oil until tender. The same people are also adamant about cutting out the cores before cooking. For this recipe, if you can believe it, I complicate life even more. But for good reason: when the leaves are pulled from the sprouts, tossed into the pan like a rainfall of rose petals, sautéed until soft and beginning to brown, then flecked with bacon, you've just made candy.

1 pound/500 g Brussels sprouts
8 strips bacon
2 tablespoons unsalted butter
1 tablespoon olive oil
Salt and pepper

Core the sprouts and peel off the leaves one by one, discarding the tight, inner-most heads. Heat a sauté pan and fry the bacon until crisp; remove to paper towels to drain. Pour all but 1 tablespoon of fat from the pan. Add the butter and oil, then toss in the sprout leaves. Sauté until tender, 15 to 20 minutes. Season with salt and pepper. Crumble over the bacon, and serve.

APPLE CABBAGE

[*Serves 6*]

*T*his rendition of braised cabbage makes the most of its purple appearance and rich taste: the smoke of bacon, the tart/sweet of apple, and the depth of wine and stock make a complex and full-flavored dish that glistens like a giant jewel. It's perfect with pork or roasted game birds.

1 pound/500 g red cabbage (about ¼ medium cabbage), cored
1 tablespoon vegetable oil
4 ounces/60 g smoky bacon, cut into pieces
1 small onion, chopped
1 tablespoon red wine vinegar
½ cup/125 ml red wine
½ cup/125 ml beef stock
2 garlic cloves, crushed
1 bay leaf
Salt and pepper
2 tablespoons unsalted butter
2 tablespoons sugar
2 tart apples, peeled, cored, and diced

Bring a large pot of salted water to a boil. Shred the cabbage with a large knife, removing any tough ribs as you go. Blanch in the boiling water for 5 minutes, drain, rinse under ice-cold water, and drain well again. The cabbage will have turned a shocking electric blue. The next step will return it to its original color.

Heat the oil in a large pot. Add the bacon and onion. Cook until the bacon is brown and the onion soft, about 10 minutes. Add the cabbage, and pour over the vinegar, wine, and stock. Poke in the garlic and bay leaf. Season with salt and pepper. Bring to a simmer, cover halfway with a lid, and cook until tender, 30 to 40 minutes.

Meanwhile, melt the butter with the sugar in a pan. Sauté the apples until golden, about 10 minutes. Stir into the cabbage. Check the seasonings. Serve warm.

LIME-BUTTER BROCCOLI

[*Serves 4*]

This is brilliant idea and I'm sorry I can't give credit, because I have no idea where I got the recipe. Whatever its origins, broccoli with lime is a real find, good alongside Almond Sole (page 84) or other fish dishes.

---

1 cup/250 ml white wine
Grated zest and juice of 1 lime
2 shallots, minced
Salt and pepper to taste
2 heads broccoli, broken into bouquets
¼ cup/60 g unsalted butter, cut into bits

Bring a large pot of salted water to boil for the broccoli. Meanwhile, put the wine, lime juice (reserve the zest), shallots, salt, and pepper in a small sauccpan and boil to reduce by half, about 7 minutes.

When the water boils, cook the broccoli in it until tender. Drain, and immediatcly rinse under ice-cold water to preserve the color. Drain well.

Whisk the butter, a few pieces at a time, into the reduced wine mixture. Stir in the lime zest, check the seasonings, and toss with the broccoli. Serve warm.

JERUSALEM ARTICHOKES
WITH WALNUT AND DILL

[*Serves 4*]

Whoever decided that walnut and dill belong together was a genius. Here, against the nutty background of Jerusalem artichokes, sautéed al dente so that they keep a bit of bite, they are grand. Try the dish warm with Wine Sausages (page 103), or serve at room temperature on the buffet table—and watch them go.

1 pound/500 g Jerusalem artichokes
2 tablespoons unsalted butter
Salt and pepper
2 tablespoons walnut oil
½ cup/60 g roughly crushed walnuts
2 to 3 tablespoons chopped fresh dill
Lemon juice to taste

Peel the artichokes and slice paper-thin with a knife or mandoline. Heat the butter to foaming in a sauté pan, add the artichoke slices, and season with salt and pepper. Sauté until they start softening and browning but still have a little bite, just over 5 minutes. Pour over the oil and heat through gently, then remove from the heat and stir in the walnuts and dill. Squeeze on lemon juice to taste and adjust the seasonings. Serve warm or at room temperature.

RED ONION BEETS

[*Serves 4*]

*B*eet fan that I am, a simple bowl of buttered slices, or even a jar of the pickled wedges and a fork, makes me happy. This recipe is the best of both worlds. The hint of acidity from the vinegar and capers, strewn through the soft, ruby-hued strands of onion and the sweet bites of beet, gives perfect balance.

2 tablespoons olive oil
1 pound/500 g red onions, very thinly sliced
2 tablespoons red wine vinegar
1 pound/500 g cooked beets, diced
Salt and pepper
3 to 4 tablespoons drained capers

Heat the oil in a sauté pan over medium heat. Fry the onions until very soft but not coloring, about 20 minutes. Stir in the vinegar and add the beets, tossing to coat. Season with salt and pepper, then scatter over the capers. Serve warm.

FRUIT AND NUTS CAULIFLOWER

[*Serves 4*]

One of these days when you're not coating cauliflower in a warm, flowing cheese sauce, or dipping crunchy raw bouquets into mayonnaise, try this. The combination is unlikely, but festive: matchsticks of apricot, pinches of sticky black prune, golden raisins, tiger-eyed pistachios, toasted pine nuts, crumbled walnuts, diced sweet date, all kaleidoscoped against a buttery cauliflower canvas. It seems positively commissioned for Hay Ham (page 142) or any other celebratory ham.

1 tablespoon white wine vinegar
1 head cauliflower (about 2 pounds/1 kg), broken into small bouquets
½ cup/60 g mixed nuts (pine nuts, pistachios, walnuts, hazelnuts, and peanuts)
½ cup/60 g mixed dried fruit (apricots, raisins, prunes, and dates)
¼ cup/60 g unsalted butter
Salt and pepper

Add the vinegar to a large pot of salted water and bring to a boil. Add the cauliflower bouquets and cook until al dente, 7 to 8 minutes. Drain, and rinse under cold water to stop the cooking; drain again.

Meanwhile, heat a sauté pan over medium heat and brown the nuts until they begin to emit a perfume, 3 to 5 minutes. Add the dried fruit and butter; heat until the butter melts.

Stir the cauliflower into the butter mixture to coat and warm through. Season with salt and pepper. Serve.

ZUCCHINI FONDUE

[*Serves 4*]

S ometimes it's the smallest detail that makes or breaks a dish. That's the case here. When zucchini is sliced paper-thin and sautéed, it becomes another vegetable entirely: meltingly soft buttery ruffles of green and cream. I don't even add herbs, so perfect I think this tastes as is, but you go ahead if you want.

2 pounds/1 kg small zucchini
2 tablespoons olive oil
2 to 3 tablespoons unsalted butter
Salt and pepper

Trim the zucchini and slice into paper-thin rounds with a very sharp knife, or with a mandoline. Heat the oil and butter in a sauté pan over medium heat and add the zucchini. Cook, tossing occasionally, until wilted, ruffled, and just beginning to brown, 10 to 15 minutes. Season with salt and pepper, and serve.

BALSAMIC CHESTNUTS

[*Serves 4*]

*B*efore vacuum-packed chestnuts were available, this recipe would have been an ordeal. But now that you can buy them ready-peeled and cooked, this preparation is ultra-simple: quick gratification for when a roasted bird begs for the fudgy, matte density of the chestnut tree's fine fruit.

2 to 3 tablespoons unsalted butter
1 pound/500 g vacuum-packed cooked, peeled chestnuts
2 to 3 tablespoons balsamic vinegar
Salt and pepper

Melt the butter in a sauté pan. Add the chestnuts and toss to coat and heat through, about 2 minutes. Add the vinegar and boil, stirring, until reduced to a glaze, just a minute or two. Season with salt and pepper. Serve hot.

DESSERTS

The French, like us, don't always serve dessert; it's a course to add to the menu on a special night, and even then some prefer to replace their sweet with cheese. When I go the cheese route, I serve, say, three to five different kinds, depending on how many people will be at table and on what's looking good in the shop. I also look for a few interesting breads to go with them, maybe a walnut bread and a fig bread, along with a good baguette. The cheese goes on a cutting board, the bread in a basket, and everyone helps himself. Don't "steal the nose" from cheese when you serve yourself: slice the cheese according to its shape, which keeps a partly eaten piece looking good for another day and spares some poor soul from being left with nothing but a hard plank of rind.

Fruit is another easy option for ending a meal, and when it's in season (which, obviously, it should be) fresh fruit, unadorned, is hardly a cop-out. Frankly, when there are berries bursting from the market stands, it seems blasphemous to nature not to serve them. So, for example, when cherries are at their peak, heap them glamorously high in a bowl and set a small empty dish somewhere in range for pits. Let everyone eat them by the handful, dangling cherries by the stems above their mouths and flicking them in with their tongues. A pyramid of clementines with a plate of sticky-sweet dates takes the gloom from the winter drill of apples. And, in autumn, why not an arrangement? Pear wedges, fresh pineapple, and walnuts are good mates. By "arrangement," incidentally, I mean fruits held in the hands about six inches above a platter and let to fall and nestle among themselves as they will.

Now, about "real" desserts. Since bakeries and pastry shops in France are good and abundant, French home cooks are often precisely that: cooks, not bakers. Follow suit, if you like. Instead of sweating over dessert when time is short, offer a bought apricot tart, or sorbet with a plate of pastry-shop tuiles. I would forgo those individual desserts with the plastic belts around their midriffs, or anything else that screams: I'm bought! Not to hide the fact that I don't deserve the credit for dessert, mind you, but because dessert should be in tune with the rest of the meal; it should resemble the kind of food I make at home, not look like an edible amusement-park ride.

Of course, I'm biased. I don't have a sweet tooth and I'm not a perfectionist, so desserts for me must be light, small, and extraordinarily simple to make. In this chapter, that's what you'll find: easy, simple, tasty sweet endings.

FIREPLACE CAMEMBERT

[*Serves 2*]

I'm seriously considering renting a room in a rustic lodge just so I can finally do this Camembert properly. However, I'll be damned if I change the title of the recipe just because I'm stuck for now doing it in the oven. If you don't have Pernod in the cupboard, white wine works too.

One 8-ounce/250-g Camembert
2 tablespoons Pernod or other anise-flavored liquour

Remove the Camembert from its box, unwrap, and set on a piece of foil. Perforate the top of the cheese a few times with a fork, then sprinkle over the Pernod, letting it trickle into the holes. Close the foil, seal well, and nudge the package into the incandescent coals of your fireplace.

Okay, okay, so put it in a preheated oven at 400°F/200°C for 10 minutes. You want the cheese to be soft and melting, but not gushing all over your plate; think fondue, but with form. When it's ready, pull the Camembert from the fire, peel back the foil, and slit the surface. Eat the gooey hot cheese smeared onto rips of crusty bread.

CHEESE CREAMS

[*Serves 6*]

I tried traditional *coeurs à la crème,* beaten egg whites and whipped cream folded together with fresh cheese, and I just didn't like them. However, the essence of the idea still appealed, something fresh, slightly tangy, cheesy, plain, something to dribble honey and scatter cracked walnuts over, or to serve with a fresh blackberry sauce (that is: 2 parts berries puréed, strained, and sweetened with sugar to 1 part whole berries), or fresh peach or apricot slices, or even a dried fruit compote. So, I fiddled around. This combination of yogurt, cream cheese, mascarpone, and heavy cream gives just the result I'd dreamt of: pure white, light (but not in a fluffy way), complex in taste, barely sweet, and the pinnacle of simplicity to make. Never mind the traditional perforated heart-shaped molds (I don't have them either). Ramekins (below) work with this version, as do paper cups. Or, you could line a conical sieve with the cloth and make a giant pyramid. Just wait until you see walnuts and honey cascading down that.

One 3-ounce/100-g package cream cheese
1 cup/250 g thick plain yogurt, preferably sheep's or goat's milk
½ cup/125 g mascarpone cheese
½ cup/125 ml heavy cream
2 tablespoons confectioners' sugar, or more to taste
2 teaspoons lemon juice

Beat the cream cheese in a bowl until soft. Beat in the yogurt and mascarpone until smooth. Finally, beat in the cream. Whisk in the sugar and lemon juice to taste.

Line six ½-cup/125-ml molds, or a large bowl, with a double layer of dry muslin (or cheesecloth). Spoon in the cheese-cream mixture and smooth the top. Fold over the muslin, press down slightly, and refrigerate overnight. Unmold to serve with the topping of your choice (see above for ideas).

PARMESAN AND PINK PEPPER STRAWBERRIES

*P*eople are always surprised by this combination: sweet, salty, followed by hot. It's an idea, really, more than a recipe, and so I've left out quantities, because you're hardly going to start counting out peppercorns per handful of berries. Trust your tongue.

Ripe strawberries, hulled and halved or sliced
Aged Parmigiano-Reggiano
Pepper
Pink peppercorns, crushed

Arrange the berries in serving bowls. Slice over small curls of Parmigiano-Reggiano using a vegetable peeler. Grind on black pepper. Scatter over crushed pink peppercorns. Serve.

ROSEMARY APRICOTS

[*Serves 6*]

One of life's small perfections: two sunny apricot halves beaming up with a shiny, warm pool of rosemary-perfumed syrup spooned around them. I peel the fruit because it's a crime to leave that stunning apricot color hidden beneath the skin. Also, I make them at the last minute, because if left to cool in their syrup, the apricots overcook and start to loose their perfect fanny shape. They're best eaten warm anyway.

6 firm ripe apricots
1 cup/200 g sugar
Leaves from 1 branch rosemary

Bring a fairly large saucepan of water to the boil. Etch an X in the bottom of each apricot. Plunge 3 at a time into the water and count to 12. Immediately remove and rinse under ice-cold water to cool completely. Peel, halve, and pit.

Gently heat the sugar in a sauté pan with ½ cup/125 ml water and the rosemary. Once the sugar has dissolved, bring to a simmer. Lay in the apricots, fanny side down, and poach until just tender, about 3 minutes. Don't let them get too soft.

Remove the fruit with a perforated spoon and lay two halves on each serving plate. Boil the cooking liquid down to syrup, about 5 minutes. Spoon around the apricots and serve immediately.

SPARKLING RED SOUP

[*Serves 4*]

I too read the ingredients list and thought, "Ho-hum, more or less berries." But what a shock when I put it all together and found they'd metamorphosed into a stunning scarlet soup, dazzling with gems of fruit, and set a-fizz with a shot of sparkling wine. It's gorgeous without the wine too, not as festive maybe, but then you can eat the leftovers for breakfast. This recipe is based on one by Raymond Blanc, a French chef who has made his career in England.

½ pound/250 g raspberries
½ pound/250 g strawberries
½ cup/100 g sugar, or more to taste
Juice of ½ lemon
1 pound/500 g mixed soft fruit (raspberries, strawberries, blackberries,
  blueberries, sliced peaches, red currants, diced mango, and so on)
A handful of mint leaves, chopped
About ½ cup/125 ml sparkling wine

Purée the raspberries and strawberries. Press through a sieve. Add the sugar and lemon juice. Chill the sauce and the mixed fruit separately for at least 2 hours.

To serve, stir the fruit into the purée. Ladle into soup plates. Scatter over the mint. Pass the bottle of sparkling wine around the table, letting everyone pour a glug into his bowl and watch it fizz. Pour what's left into your glasses, obviously.

NUTTY FIGS

[*Serves 4*]

Made with tiny purple figs, these were too cute for words: fruit slit to open like the beaks of baby birds and into each mouth poked a fragrant, nutty nubbin. These can be made as early in the day as you want, for broiling at the last minute. Then all they need is a dollop of cream. Try them with peach or apricot halves too, the nut mixture in the middle where the pit used to be.

8 small figs or 4 large ones
2 tablespoons unsalted butter, softened
2 tablespoons sugar
¼ cup/30 g ground pistachios or other nuts

Preheat the oven to broil. Cut a cross from the top about three-quarters of the way down into the figs. Mash together the butter, sugar, and ground pistachios. Divide into as many balls as you have figs, and poke one into the mouth of each. Broil 8 to 10 minutes, until the nut mixture is golden and the figs hot. Serve with whipped cream or crème fraîche.

SPICED WINE PEARS

[*Serves 6*]

*P*oached pears always looked so sophisticated to me that I never dared make them. Silly me. I mean, if you can make a cup of tea, you can poach a pear. I like mine well spiced, but even if you have just one or two of those suggested below on hand, your simmered fruits glazed in glossy wine-red robes will be impressive. I say six pears serves six, but if they're especially large, maybe you want to make only three and give each person half, preferably with a scoop of cinnamon ice cream.

6 pears
1 strip orange peel
One 750-ml bottle red wine
¾ cup/150 g sugar
1 cinnamon stick
1 tablespoon peppercorns
2 cardamom pods
2 cloves
2 star anise

Peel the pears. Remove any white pith from the back of the orange peel with a sharp knife. In a large saucepan, gently heat the wine and sugar. Once the sugar has dissolved, add the orange peel and the spices and bring to a boil. Lower in the pears and simmer, turning once or twice, until tender, about 20 minutes.

Remove the pot from the heat and let the pears cool in the syrup. Or, to serve warm, remove the pears to plates, cutting a sliver from the bottom so they'll stand straight. Strain the liquid into a wide saucepan and boil down to a light syrup, about 10 minutes. Spoon over the pears and serve.

FLAMBÉED BANANAS

[*Serves 4*]

*N*ot new, but it's the best last-minute, bail-out dessert of all time. I'll use any bananas I can get my hands on, but some say the flavor is improved when they're slightly overripe. Some also think this can use more rum, but that's a matter (one would like to think) of taste. If you use apple slices and calvados instead of bananas and rum, you have another great dessert. Diced (slightly overripe) pears, *sans* booze, are also heavenly. And any of these variations parceled and baked in a few layers of crisp filo pastry, or simply used to fill a pre-baked tart shell, will send you swooning (see Pear Purses, page 209, for more details). Don't forget the praline ice cream losing its cool alongside.

¼ cup/60 g unsalted butter
¼ cup/50 g sugar
4 medium bananas
¼ cup/60 g rum

Melt the butter and sugar together in a frying pan over medium heat until they turn to caramel, about 5 minutes.

Peel and slice the bananas lengthwise in half. Add them to the pan, and cook, turning once, until slightly softened and well coated with the caramel, another 5 minutes. (You might want to do this in two batches if you're pressed for space in the frying pan. Then just combine the two before the next step.)

Pour the rum over the bananas and carefully set it alight. When the flame dies, arrange the bananas on dessert plates, spoon some sauce over, and serve immediately.

French Food at Home

HOT PASSION FRUIT SOUFFLÉS

*Y*ou only *think* you're too full for dessert. Besides, this is a particularly light soufflé without a pastry-cream base—which also means that it takes less time to prepare. Passion fruit has a tangy, tropical taste, practically citrus. But, if you can't find passion fruit, use raspberries instead. It will be different, of course, but equally good, cotton-candy colored with lipstick-red juice trickling through. For the berry version, purée about 2 cups/250 g raspberries, strain through a sieve, measure out ¾ cup/175 ml juice, and proceed with the recipe. Cut the sugar back a bit, because raspberry juice is sweeter than that of passion fruit.

12 to 16 passion fruit, depending on size and quality
2 egg yolks
6 tablespoons sugar
4 egg whites
Confectioners' sugar to taste

Preheat the oven to 425°F/220°C. Butter six ½-cup/125 ml ramekins and stick them in the freezer. Halve the passion fruits, scoop out the flesh, and press through a sieve to extract the juice; you need ¾ cup/175 ml.

Beat the yolks with 2 tablespoons of the sugar in a small bowl until pale and thick, then whisk in ¼ cup/60 ml of the passion fruit juice. Beat the whites, add the remaining 4 tablespoons sugar and beat to a stiff meringue. Take a spoonful out and stir it into the yolk mixture, then pour the yolk mixture back over into the meringue and fold together gently.

Fill the ramekins and smooth the tops with a knife. Run a finger around the inside lip so that they'll rise evenly. Bake until they've puffed up high and turned golden on top, about 10 minutes. While the soufflés bake, pour the remaining fruit juice into a saucepan, boil to thicken somewhat, and sweeten to taste with confectioners' sugar. Transfer to a small bowl for serving.

Remove the soufflés from the oven and speed them to the table, making sure everybody slits open the tops with their spoons and pours in some of that luscious, deep yellow passion fruit sauce.

COFFEE POTS

[*Serves 6*]

One of the simplest and best desserts I know. My creamy coffee pots are based on food writer Patricia Wells' lemon version, wherein fresh lemon or lime juice replaces the wincingly strong coffee below (added to the sugar—upped to ½ cup/100 g in the lemon case—rather than boiled with the milk). Both ways, they are unsurpassed: polished in flavor and sublimely smooth in texture.

1½ cups/375 ml cream
½ cup/125 ml very strong coffee
¼ cup/60 g sugar
6 egg yolks

Preheat the oven to 325°F/160°C. Bring the cream and coffee to a boil in a saucepan. Meanwhile, beat the sugar and egg yolks together in a bowl until light and fluffy. If you'd thought of adding a shot of alcohol or other flavoring, this is the time.

Slowly pour the scalded coffee milk into the egg mixture, whisking constantly. Strain into six ½-cup/125-ml ramekins. Skim off any foam that forms on top (if it bothers you). Set the ramekins into a baking dish and pour around boiling water to come halfway up their sides.

Bake until just set, about 30 minutes. Remove from the oven and cool, then refrigerate for several hours, or overnight, before serving.

CHICKEN MILK

[*Makes 4 cups/1 liter*]

*I*f you call *lait de poule* "eggnog," which is what this is, you don't get the joke. But if you translate the French appellation directly—chicken milk—it freaks everybody out. And that, if you ask me, would be enough to make this drinking dessert worth serving even if it weren't its thick, cool, smooth, sweet self, whispering hints of vanilla bean, nutmeg, and rum. Serve it before, after, with, or as dessert. And don't hesitate to play around with flavorings. Orange flower water is a good variation.

4 cups/1 l whole milk
1 vanilla bean, split
Pinch of freshly grated nutmeg, or to taste
4 egg yolks
4 to 6 tablespoons sugar
2 to 4 tablespoons dark rum (optional)

Pour the milk into a saucepan and scrape the seeds from the vanilla pod into it. Add the pod to the pot too, and grind in some nutmeg. Heat gently just to the boiling point. Remove from the heat, cover, and infuse for 10 minutes.

Meanwhile, beat together the yolks and sugar in a bowl. Pour the warm milk over, whisking constantly. Return to the heat and whisk until slightly thickened, 3 to 5 minutes. Taste and adjust the sugar and nutmeg. Chill. Remove the vanilla bean and lace with rum, if you like, before serving.

LOST BREAD

[*Serves 4*]

*S*ounds like a fairy tale's tragedy, doesn't it? Well, in a way it is, since fool-ishly we've allowed *pain perdu* to fall out of fashion. But this dessert is worth hanging on to, especially done like this: sugary, hot, crisp, soft egg-bread toast, blackened outside with a milky white middle like a giant roasted marsh-mallow, and, in this case, trailing fumes of tangy liquored orange through the air. If the occasion is extra special, you might want to make candied orange peel for garnish: Remove the peel from an orange with a sharp knife, then remove all the white pith from the back. Slice the peel into fine julienne and cover with cold water in a saucepan. Bring to a boil, boil 5 minutes, and strain. Then dissolve a heaping tablespoon of sugar in 2 tablespoons of fresh water in that same saucepan. Put in the blanched julienne, and boil gently until the liquid has evap-orated and the orange is coated, glistening, and candied, about 10 minutes. Drain on a wire rack, and store in an airtight container until using.

½ cup/125 ml orange juice
6 tablespoons sugar
1½ teaspoons cornstarch
Grated zest of 1 orange
1 to 2 teaspoons orange liqueur (optional)
¼ cup/60 g cold unsalted butter, cut into bits
1½ cups/375 ml milk
1 teaspoon vanilla extract
4 thick slices egg bread, such as brioche or challah, preferably day-old
2 eggs

First make the sauce: Whisk together the orange juice, 2 tablespoons of the sugar, and the cornstarch in a saucepan. Bring slowly to a boil, stirring con-stantly, until it thickens enough to coat a spoon, about 5 minutes. Whisk in the zest and the orange liqueur, if using. Remove from the heat and whisk in half the butter, a piece at a time, to make it glossy. Set aside.

Put the oven rack at the highest notch and preheat the oven to broil. Combine the milk and vanilla in a shallow dish and soak the bread in it for about 10 minutes, turning once so that it absorbs the milk evenly. Beat the eggs with 2 more tablespoons of the sugar in a bowl.

Heat the remaining butter in a skillet. Remove the bread from the milk and dip into the eggs to coat. Fry until well browned (a little black doesn't hurt either) and crispy edged, about 5 minutes per side. Transfer the fried bread slices to a baking sheet and sprinkle the tops with the remaining 2 tablespoons sugar. Broil quickly to caramelize the tops, about 2 minutes (this can also be the job of a blowtorch, if you have one). Remove the toasts to serving plates. Spoon around the sauce, garnish with candied orange if you've made it, and serve.

ICED NOUGAT CUBES

[*Serves 8 generously*]

This is a winter wonderland for the mouth: frosty white, creamy cubes studded with bright candied fruit, chewy flecks of dried fruit, toasted almonds, crushed praline, emerald green pistachios. . . . The most irresistible shape for them is perfect blocks, so I make the nougat in a flat cake pan and slice to serve. Iced nougat cubes need no accompaniment, but whoever said we have to *need* one to have one? Try mango or raspberry *coulis:* simply purée and strain the fresh fruit, then sweeten it with a little confectioners' sugar. Also, feel free to use the orange sauce from Lost Bread (page 201) or a caramel sauce.

½ cup/75 g chopped mixed dried fruit, such as raisins, apricots, and figs
½ cup/100 g chopped candied fruit, such as orange peel, pineapple, and cherries
2 tablespoons Cointreau, rum, or other alcohol (optional)
¼ cup/35 g skinned whole almonds
¼ cup/20 g slivered almonds
6 tablespoons sugar
¼ cup/30 g pistachios, chopped
½ cup/125 g mascarpone cheese
1 cup/250 ml heavy cream
3 egg whites

Line a square or rectangular cake pan with plastic wrap. Combine the dried and candied fruits in a bowl and sprinkle over the Cointreau. Leave to macerate while you toast the whole almonds in a dry frying pan, stirring, until golden, about 10 minutes. Set aside. Now toast the sliced almonds, stirring, until lightly golden, about 5 minutes. Sprinkle over 2 tablespoons of the sugar, and continue stirring until melted and caramelized, about 2 minutes. Spread on a baking sheet and leave a few minutes to harden, then chop into raisin-sized pieces.

Mix all the nuts in with the fruit. Add the mascarpone and mix well with your fingers. Whip the heavy cream and set aside.

Set a large metal bowl over a pan of simmering water on low heat. Put in the egg whites and the remaining 4 tablespoons sugar and whisk until thick (like whipped cream) and glossy, about 5 minutes. Remove the bowl from the heat. Fold the whipped cream into the fruit mixture, then fold in the egg whites. Pour into the lined pan, cover with plastic wrap, and freeze for 12 hours.

To serve, flip the iced nougat onto a cutting surface and slice into neat ice cube–sized pieces. Serve each person about 3, either plain or in a pool of sauce.

WHITE CHOCOLATE CREAMS

[*Serves 4 to 6*]

No matter what you think of white chocolate (I think those thoughts too) this really is good: wild, thick, unctuous drifts of smooth Cointreau-flavored chocolate cream. It takes seconds to whip up and the results are marvelous. White chocolate is my favorite here, but you can use milk chocolate or dark chocolate instead. Try another flavoring, like vanilla or rum, instead of Cointreau. And, crème fraîche or sour cream rushes to the rescue if you can't find mascarpone. Serve the creams in small ramekins, teacups, or demitasses.

¼ pound/125 g white chocolate
¼ cup/60 ml heavy cream
1 cup/250 g mascarpone cheese
2 teaspoons Cointreau or Grand Marnier (optional)

Melt the chocolate very gently in the heavy cream in a bowl or double boiler over hot, not boiling, water. Remove from the heat and cool to room temperature. Whisk in the mascarpone until smooth. Stir in the Cointreau (whisking at this point would cause curdling). Transfer to small molds, cover, and refrigerate for several hours before serving.

THE LEMON TART OF MY DREAMS

[*Makes one 8-inch/20-cm tart*]

There are more recipes for lemon tart out there than you can shake a fork at. Some have candied lemon slices afloat on top like so many shipwrecked unicycles; others, for reasons I cannot divine, are hell-bent on involving ground almonds, and yet others have emerged from my hopeful oven all a-wiggle with butter. But all I want when I want lemon tart is the plainest possible thing: flat, smooth, and puckering with intense lemon flavor. So that's why another lemon tart recipe simply had to be.

2 eggs
2 egg yolks
⅔ cup/135 g sugar, or more to taste
Grated zest of 2 lemons
⅔ cup/160 ml lemon juice (from about 3 large lemons)
½ cup/125 ml crème fraîche, sour cream, or heavy cream
One 8-inch/20-cm Sweet Pastry shell (page 219), prebaked
Confectioners' sugar

Preheat the oven to 350°F/175°C. Beat together the eggs, yolks, and sugar in a bowl. Add the lemon zest and juice, mixing well. Whisk in the cream. Pour into the prebaked tart shell. Skim off any surface foam.

Bake until just set, 15 to 20 minutes. Let cool, dust with confectioners' sugar, and serve.

WALNUT TART

[*Makes one 10-inch/25-cm tart*]

*T*hroughout the cooler months, a bag of walnuts always hangs on the back of my kitchen door. Sometimes I have phases of going through about one a week: cracking them for salads, grinding them for cakes, crushing them with garlic and oil for meat sauce, or splitting them into halves for desserts such as this one. What a sight it is: a flat tart brimming with a chaos of walnuts all swathed in thick, buttery caramel.

1½ cups/300 g sugar
2 tablespoons unsalted butter
1 cup/250 ml heavy cream
About ½ pound/250 g walnut halves
One 10-inch/25-cm Sweet Pastry shell (page 219), prebaked

Put the sugar and butter in a heavy saucepan. Gently heat, stirring, until the sugar has dissolved and turned a rich caramel color, about 15 minutes. Add the cream. This will immediately cause the sugar to seize and you to panic, but don't: just keep stirring until the caramel lump melts again. Remove from the heat, then stir in the walnut halves. Pour into the prepared tart shell and let sit at room temperature until firm, about 3 hours.

HOT CHOCOLATE

[*Serves 4 to 6*]

You can indeed get away with serving this for dessert, and this alone, although a few madeleines (page 214) on the side never hurts. A rich, super chocolaty, smooth, warming drink like this is just the kind of thing I appreciate after a winter dinner. It's also great, though, in the afternoons when you come in from a nippy walk.

4 cups/1 l whole milk
1 cup/250 ml heavy cream
3 ounces/80 g best-quality dark chocolate
4 tablespoons unsweetened cocoa powder
4 tablespoons sugar

Put the milk, cream, and chocolate in a saucepan and heat gently until the chocolate has melted. Combine the cocoa and sugar in a small bowl and stir in just a bit of the milk mixture to make a smooth paste, then stir that paste back into the warm milk. Continue heating, now whisking constantly, until the chocolate milk is hot and frothy. Ladle into cups, and serve.

PEAR PURSES

*W*rapping buttery soft, sweetened sautéed fruit such as apples, pears, bananas, or peaches in pastry and baking it in the form of small purses is really very speedy, and the result will make you feel like a real pro. Serve with crème fraîche on the side.

4 large ripe pears, peeled and cored
2 tablespoons unsalted butter, plus more for brushing
4 tablespoons sugar
3 sheets filo pastry, thawed according to package instructions

Cut the pears into roughly ½-inch/1-cm cubes. Heat the butter in a skillet until foaming and add the pears. Cook until their juices have run and then evaporated to almost nothing, 15 to 20 minutes. Sprinkle over the sugar and cook until it starts to caramelize and coat the pears, 10 to 15 minutes longer.

Preheat the oven to 400°F/200°C. Melt an additional tablespoon or so of butter for brushing the filo. Lay out one sheet and brush with butter. Lay a second on top and brush again. Lay on the third and brush a final time. Cut into 4 rectangles.

Spoon some of the pear mixture into the center of each and bundle up into a purse, or fold into a package. Set on a nonstick baking sheet. Brush the tops with butter. Bake until the pastry is crisp and golden and the centers hot, about 10 minutes. Serve warm.

PAPER-THIN PEACH TARTS

[*Serves 4*]

*O*nce you get the hang of these speedy tarts, you can do endless variations, including savory. The method below is for warm tarts, best suited to combinations such as fig slices, honey, and pine nuts; sautéed cinnamon apples or bananas; caramelized onion. For cold tarts, I recommend prebaking the pastry circles until crisp and golden, about 10 minutes. Then just before serving, put anything you want on them: mascarpone and honey with blueberries, rhubarb compote with sliced strawberries, lemon curd, and so on.

About 3 small ripe peaches
6 sheets filo pastry, thawed according to package instructions
2 tablespoons unsalted butter, melted
4 teaspoons sugar, or more to taste

Preheat the oven to 400°F/200°C. Bring a large pot of water to the boil. Score an X in the bottom of each peach and plunge into the water. Count to 12, remove the peaches, and plunge them into ice-cold water. Peel, halve lengthwise, and slice into thin half-moons.

Brush a sheet of filo with melted butter and lay another sheet on top. Continue until you've got a stack, 6 sheets thick. From this, cut four 4- to 5-inch/10- to 13-cm circles with the tip of a knife, perhaps working around a saucer as a guide. Brush the tops with melted butter and sprinkle over half the sugar. Lay on peach slices in an overlapping ring on each one. Sprinkle with the remaining sugar.

Bake the tarts until the filo is crisp and the peaches warm, about 15 minutes.

THE SECRETS OF TARTE TATIN

I understand why most recipes for tarte Tatin don't look like the pictures promise. It's all method, this dessert, and there are far too many details to cram into recipe form, so they're usually left out. It's better to learn tarte Tatin standing at the stove with someone walking you through it: then you catch all the tricks. So let's do it that way. First, though, you need a disk of Sweet Pastry (page 219) chilling in the fridge.

Apple choice is all-important: you need a not overly juicy variety, such as Royal Gala or Golden Delicious, and you need a lot of them, 12 to 14 anyway, for a 12- to 14-inch/30- to 36 cm tarte pan or cast-iron skillet. Drying the apples a bit before making the tart is worth the extra time because they'll produce less juice during cooking, plus they'll shrink somewhat and become supple, which allows you to fit more into the pan. So turn the oven on to 200°F/100°C. Peel, core, and halve the apples, lay them right in on the oven racks, and leave for 1 to 1½ hours, while you do something else. When they're just dry to the touch and slightly colored, remove. Increase the heat to 425°F/220°C.

Now, put ¾ cup/175 g unsalted butter and 2 cups/400 g sugar in your pan over medium heat. Let them melt together without stirring. The mixture won't become liquid right away—first it will get slushy, in about 5 minutes. Now you can begin stirring occasionally. The slush will come to a boil, then transform into a stiff, white froth, and eventually become mealy. All this, however strange looking, is normal, so don't worry. Once it has passed through those stages, the mixture will finally melt into a rich, liquid caramel. It takes about 20 to 30 minutes total, and at this point it is dangerously hot, so be careful with the next step.

Add the apple halves to the pan: The best way I've found to do this is to lay a wooden spoon across the center of the pan, balanced on the rim. Now, lean one apple half up against it, core side against the spoon, running horizontally. Lay another apple half in the same way behind it, and continue around in a circle making concentric rings. Remove the spoon and fill the center with apples in the same position. Pack them as tight as you can. When no more apples fit, know that an additional 2 to 3 halves *will* eventually: once the apples have been cooking for a while, gaps appear. So have them at the ready to poke in. Cook the apples in the pan for 20 minutes.

By this time, the apples will be nicely caramelized on one side. Using a fork and spoon, carefully turn them over, one at a time, so that the other side can caramelize too. Don't worry if some apples break a little, because you're turning them mooshy side down, the good side up once it's flipped. Once turned, continue cooking until the apples are nicely colored on the other side, about 20 minutes longer.

As the cooking reaches its final stretch and the caramel boils down to a thick syrup around the apples, sticking is possible. Not, however, if you take hold of the pan with both oven-mitted hands and give it a twist or two like a steering wheel. The apples will unstick and spin together in the pan. I do this once or twice during cooking just to reassure myself.

Time to take the pastry from the fridge. Roll it to a circle the size of the pan, then lay it over the apples, tucking it snugly into the edges like a blanket. Now slip the pan into the oven and bake until the pastry is golden and crisp, 15 to 20 minutes. Remove from the oven and cool 10 minutes before turning out.

Or, if you don't plan to serve the tart for a few hours, leave it in the pan. To serve, set the pan on the burner for a few minutes to loosen the caramel. You know it's ready when you take the pan by both oven-mitted hands again, give it a twist, and feel the apples move.

Set a large plate on top of the crust and flip the whole thing over. It should be caramelized, glossy, and majestic, begging to be shown off in candlelight. Waltz it on in to the table, beaming graciously, and not trying to hide your own awe. If anyone asks for ice cream, you can't hear them. Crème fraîche is fine, but as you'll soon taste, a tarte Tatin this grand can stand alone. This will serve 8 to 10.

COCONUT CAKES

[*Makes about 16 small cakes*]

*M*y general lack of interest in sweets clashes head-on with my fetish for nuts in the face of these teensy flat rectangular cakes, slightly crisp at the edges, chewy outside, dense, and wettish in the center. Classically—that is, when they're made with ground almonds—they're known as *financiers,* and in that form began my love affair with the cakes. Not long afterward, I found myself with a squat two-kilo bag of hazelnuts in the cupboard, so then I got on that kick: hazelnut cakes galore. And then, along came a packet of coconut. It spurred this version, which is the living end. As you can see, it is in fact so good that it bumped the classical almonds right out of the recipe title. But please try all three versions; each has its own charm. And, if you don't have the classic shallow rectangular molds, simply use some other small mold, such as muffin or baba tins, filled partway.

⅔ cup/160 g unsalted butter
1½ cups/200 g confectioners' sugar
1 cup/90 g shredded coconut
½ cup/60 g all-purpose flour
5 egg whites
1 teaspoon vanilla extract

Preheat the oven to 450°F/230°C. Melt the butter in a saucepan and pour into a small bowl to cool. Butter and chill the molds.

Sift together the sugar, coconut, and flour. Stir in the egg whites, mixing well. Whisk in the melted butter and the vanilla.

Divide the batter among the molds. Bake 5 minutes. Reduce the heat to 400°F/ 200°C and continue baking until golden and cooked through, 10 to 15 minutes. Cool somewhat before unmolding. (If you're working in batches, don't forget to turn the oven back up.)

HONEY BABY MADELEINES

[*Makes about 48 mini madeleines*]

*T*here is a perfectly sensible reason for making these in miniature: small desserts don't count. That's reassuring when you discover that six people at dinner can make the whole lot disappear. If you're without baby madeleine tins, use a different shape altogether, such as small muffin tins, or small rectangular molds. Depending on how large you make them, the cooking time may change slightly.

¾ cup plus 1 tablespoon/200 g unsalted butter
1½ cups/200 g confectioners' sugar
5 egg whites
⅔ cup/80 g all-purpose flour
⅔ cup/80 g powdered almonds
1 tablespoon strong-tasting honey, such as chestnut

Melt the butter in a saucepan, then leave on the heat until it froths and turns hazelnut brown. While that's on the go, stir together the confectioners' sugar and egg whites in a bowl to combine, then whisk in the flour and almonds. Stir the honey into the brown butter, then pour in a thin drizzle into the flour mixture, stirring constantly. Cover and refrigerate all day, or overnight.

Preheat the oven to 400°F/200°C. Grease the tins well. Spoon in the batter to fill no more than three-quarters full, or use a piping bag for a neater job. Bake until the madeleines are nicely browned and the centers have humped up, about 10 minutes.

PINEAPPLE TUILES

[*Makes about 40 tuiles*]

These take minutes to make, but they look impressive, so don't worry about serving them plunked onto scoops of bought ice cream. What is special about these paper-thin tuiles is not only that they've got a mysterious, perky undertaste of pineapple but their golden doily-textured surface echoes in appearance the skin of a pineapple. Use them to garnish individual desserts, or serve them in a generous glossy stack with coffee. This recipe comes from chef Pascal Barbot of Astrance restaurant in Paris.

⅓ cup/75 g unsalted butter
⅓ cup/75 g roughly chopped pineapple
⅓ cup/50 g all-purpose flour
1½ cups/200 g confectioners' sugar

Preheat the oven to 350°F/175°C. Mix all the ingredients together with a blender (immersion or regular) until smooth. Drop by teaspoonfuls onto a nonstick baking sheet, spacing them well apart (I usually do only 6 at a time). Bake until you look into the oven and see flat, bubbling golden doilies, about 10 minutes. Remove.

Let the tuiles cool for half a minute on the baking sheet, then remove with a spatula. Shape, if you like, by bending the tuiles over a rolling pin for a few seconds while they're still warm and pliable. Serve or store in an airtight container.

ORANGE FLOWERY FRITTERS

*H*ow festive looking these are, all stacked up on a plate like a pyramid of small, glittery golden ornaments, showered with sugar. Orange flower flavoring suggests spring and summer, and these are spectacular that time of year, especially on a platter garnished with white blossoms. Right now, however, as I munch away at my latest batch of crisp, orangey puffs, it's nearing Christmas, so my plan is going to be replacing the orange flower water with dark rum, to taste. And then I have visions of vast heaps of fritters being popped down by my holiday visitors with Winter Wine (page 24).

½ cup/125 ml milk
2 teaspoons sugar
Pinch of salt
⅓ cup/80 g unsalted butter
1 teaspoon grated lemon zest
1 teaspoon grated orange zest
½ teaspoon orange flower water
1 cup/125 g all-purpose flour
3 eggs
4 cups/1 l peanut or vegetable oil, for frying
Confectioners' sugar

Put the milk, sugar, salt, and butter in a saucepan, along with ½ cup/125 ml water. Bring to a boil. Add the zests and orange flower water. Remove from the heat and add the flour all at once, beating with a wooden spoon until the mixture pulls away from the sides of the pan and forms a ball. Return the pan to the heat for half a minute, stirring, to dry out the paste somewhat. Remove and cool a minute or two. Add the eggs one at a time, beating vigorously after each addition to make a smooth paste.

Heat the oil in a deep-fryer or high-sided saucepan until sizzling but not smoking hot. Roll balls of dough in the palm of your hand no bigger than ¾ inch/2 cm, a few at a time, and fry, turning occasionally, until they have puffed up to double their size, cooked through completely, and colored evenly to a nice golden brown, a good 5 to 7 minutes. Remove with a slotted spoon to paper towels to drain. Sprinkle very generously with confectioners' sugar. Serve warm, or store in an airtight container to eat later.

CARAMEL MOONS

[*Makes 1 baking sheetful, for cutting into shapes*]

At Christmastime one year, French *Saveur* magazine came out with a recipe for peanut ice cream garnished with translucent peanut-packed caramel moons, as thin as stained glass. I didn't care about the ice cream, but those golden disks were mesmerizing, as if made by magic. I tried them immediately, squatting down in front of the oven, transfixed by their fantastical transformation. Then I ate three in a row. Then I started scheming up ways to make them different every time. Any kind of nut, or even a mixture of nuts, could replace the peanuts, chopped a bit if they're too big. And I'm keen on the idea of trying maple syrup or molasses instead of the honey. Be sure to serve the moons on end, propped up in ice cream or in Flambéed Bananas (page 196) for example, so that the light hits them from behind and makes them glow.

7 tablespoons heavy cream
½ cup/100 g sugar
2 tablespoons honey
About ¾ cup/100 g roasted peanuts

Preheat the oven to 375°F/190°C. Bring the cream, sugar, and honey to a boil in a saucepan. Cook 3 minutes, stirring constantly. Remove from the heat and mix in the peanuts. Pour onto a parchment-lined baking sheet (with sides), letting it spread out any which way.

Shift the pan to the oven and watch. Momentarily the mixture will turn into a mad white froth and start bubbling out to the edges of the paper. Then, in 5 to 7 minutes, the bubbles will subside to reveal a mirror-thin sheet of caramel, embedded with nuts. Remove from the oven.

Let cool a few minutes to set, without hardening completely. Then cut out circles with a metal ring, or with the tip of a knife, leaving them on the sheet to cool completely. Peel off the paper, and store in an airtight container until serving.

SWEET PASTRY

[Makes one 8-inch tart shell]

*P*rebake whenever possible is my new motto: this seems to be the guarantee for crispness. Another trick I've recently learned is how to get tarts to look perfectly pastry-shop professional without any fuss. I'm thrilled out of my wits about it, so read on.

1½ cups/200 g all-purpose flour
2 tablespoons sugar
Pinch of salt
7 tablespoons chilled unsalted butter, cut into pieces
1 egg, separated

Combine the flour, sugar, and salt in a large bowl. Add the butter and pinch into coarse crumbs with your fingers. Now make a well in the center and add the egg yolk and ¼ cup/60 ml water. Pinch just to combine, then knead only once or twice with the heel of your hand. Gather the dough into a ball and press into a disk. Wrap in plastic, and refrigerate to rest 1 hour. Refrigerate the egg white for later.

Preheat the oven to 375°F/190°C. Roll the pastry into a circle slightly larger than you think you need. Drape into the tart shell, pressing to fit, and—this is the important part—leave it draping a good inch over the outside edges. This prevents it from sinking down the sides and turning into a hard pancake.

Line the pastry with parchment and pour in dried beans, or whatever it is you use for weights. Bake until completely cooked, 15 to 20 minutes. Remove from the oven, and remove the weights. Brush the bottom with a bit of the egg white, lightly beaten to seal it and keep the crust crisp. Now, scrape around the top edge of the tart with a sharp knife to remove the pastry overhang.

Ta-da! There it is: a perfect round no-frills tart shell. Fill it as you will, with an already cooked filling, or with one which you then cook in the oven.

INDEX

Index

orange asparagus, 29–30

pea green soup, 47

pistou zucchini ribbons, 51

plain pastry, 57

scallops in velvet, 50

smoked trout rösti, 61–62

soft herb eggs, 46

toast soup, 48

fish:

almond sole, 84

bacon cod, 81

bowls, 117–18

brandade peppers, 115–16

Camembert salmon, 79

crisp vinaigrette, 86

fennel bass, 121–22

filo, in red wine sauce, 123–24

flounder in parsley, 85

herring and potato terrine, 59–60

lettuce-wrapped sea bream, 127–28

marinated tuna, 58

Parmesan flatfish, 80

pink and green papillotes, 82–83

salmon poached in olive oil, 125

sea-salt salmon, 78

smoked trout rösti, 61–62

tied, 119–20

tuna in fragrant water, 126

see also specific fish

flambéed bananas, 196

flan, vegetable, 72–73

flatfish, Parmesan, 80

flounder in parsley, 85

flower press potato chips, 13

fondue, zucchini, 185

Frenchified popcorn, 14

French toast, see lost bread

fried cheese, 54

fries, 157

fritters, orange flowery, 216–17

fruit:

dried and candied, in iced nougat cubes, 203–4

and nuts cauliflower, 184

quail, 138–39

galettes, buckwheat, 111–12

ghost soup, 49

ginger:

onion chard, 178

tomato medallions, 96

goat's cheese:

in beet stacks, 31

in spring ragout, 171

tomatoes, 26–27

goose-fat duck, 134

gougères, 15

gratin(s):

potato, 155

tomato eggplant, 166–67

green salad, 40–41

Gruyère:

in chorizette, 70–71

fried, 54

in gougères, 15

in leek tart, 67

guinea hen:

beer bird, 89

holiday hen, 135–36

ham, hay, 142

hazelnut leeks, bacon and, 28

herb lamb, 106

herbs, fresh:

in goat's cheese tomatoes, 26–27

in green salad, 40

in lettuce-wrapped sea bream, 127–28

in savory carrot cake, 109–10

in soft herb eggs, 46

in vegetable flan, 72–73

Index

Index

stocks, 108

toast, 48

sparkling red soup, 193

spice bird, 95

spiced almonds, 4

spiced wine pears, 195

spinach, lemon, 177

steak, pepper, 145–46

stocks, 108

strawberries, Parmesan and pink pepper, 191

stuffed cabbage, 140–41

summer lentils, 163–64

Swiss chard, ginger onion, 178

tabbouleh, 160

tagine, lamb, 149–50

tapenade, 7–8

tarragon chicken, 92

tart(s):

caramelized onion, 56

cherry tomato, 55–56

leek, 67

lemon tart of my dreams, 206

paper-thin peach, 210

Tatin, 211–12

walnut, 207

tartines, eggplant, 9

terrine, herring and potato, 59–60

thyme licks, 6

tied fish, 119–20

toasts, mushroom, 34–35

toast soup, 48

tomato(es):

in anchovy beef, 143–44

buttery two, 172

in chicken in vinegar, 131

cocktail, clear, 21

eggplant gratin, 166–67

and ginger medallions, 96

goat's cheese, 26–27

in ratatouille, 168–69

tarts, cherry, 55–56

torte, potato, 113–14

trout, smoked, and rösti, 61–62

tuiles:

Parmesan, 16

pineapple, 215

tuna:

in fragrant water, 126

marinated raw, 58

veal, walnut, 98–99

vegetable(s):

in fish bowls, 117–18

flan, 72–73

mixed julienne, 170

puréed, 158–59

ratatouille, 168–69

raw, in mayonnaise and crudités, 11

roasted, 165

spring ragout, 171

see also specific vegetables

vinaigrette, for onions in their skins, 32

vinegar, chicken in, 131

walnut(s):

in beet stacks, 31

in endive salad, 38

Jerusalem artichokes with dill and, 182

tart, 207

veal, 98–99

wine sausages, 103

winter wine, 24

zucchini:

fondue, 185

in ratatouille, 168–69

ribbons, pistou, 51